SACRED BUSINESS

That's a brilliant idea, but how could it possibly work in my organization?

How often do you think as you read a business book that if only you could ask the author one simple question you could transform your organization?

Capstone is creating a unique partnership between authors and readers, delivering for the first time in business book publishing a genuine after-sales service for book buyers. Simply e-mail Capstone at

capstone_publishing@msn.com

to leave your question (with details of the date and place of purchase of *Sacred Business*) and David Firth and Heather Campbell will try to answer it.

Capstone authors travel and consult extensively so we do not promise an immediate turnaround. Nevertheless, that one question answered might just jump-start your company and your career.

Capstone is more than a publisher. It is an electronic clearing house for pioneering business thinking, putting the creators of new business ideas in touch with the people who use them.

SACRED BUSINESS

*Resurrecting the
Spirit of Work*

DAVID FIRTH
and
HEATHER CAMPBELL

ODYSSEY

CAPSTONE

Copyright © David Firth and Heather Campbell 1997

First published 1997 by
Capstone Publishing Limited
Oxford Centre for Innovation
Mill Street
Oxford OX2 0JX
United Kingdom

British Library Cataloguing in Publication Data
A CIP catalogue record for this book is available from
the British Library

ISBN 1-900961-35-0

Typeset in 10/13 pt Palatino by Sue J Bushell

Printed and bound in Great Britain by
T.J. International Ltd, Padstow, Cornwall

This book is printed on acid-free paper

If you wish the world to become loving and compassionate, become loving and compassionate yourself. If you wish to diminish fear in the world, diminish your own. These are the gifts that you can give. The fear that exists between nations is a macrocosm of the fear that exists between individuals. The perception of power as external that separates nations is the same that exists between individuals; and the love, clarity and compassion that emerge within the individual that chooses consciously to align itself with its soul is the same that will bring sexes, races, nations and neighbors into harmony with each other. There is no other way ...

Gary Zukav, The Seat of the Soul

In the absence of the sacred, nothing is sacred. Everything is for sale.

Oren Lyons, Onondaga Tribal Chief

ACKNOWLEDGEMENTS

Heather

I would like to honor the four major sources of the teachings in this book: My Mother for emotional support and constant encouragement throughout my journey; Gabrielle Roth for helping me to discover my Soft power as a woman and for connecting me to my physical body; the Deer Tribe Metis Medicine Society and especially Harley Swiftdeer Reagan for the many wheels of wisdom that have provided a framework for my growth; and to all Indigenous peoples, especially the Native Americans, for creating the ceremonial path that connected me to Spirit through the power of Nature.

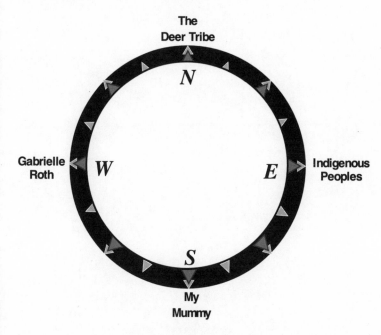

Acknowledgements wheel

David

My thanks go to Heather who helped make the writing of this book fun, strange, challenging and beautiful. It has been an exhilarating ride, which, on reflection, is a pretty fair summary of my life since I met her.

Finally, I would like to dedicate this book to my endlessly patient and loving wife Keri and our son, Ollie, who together show me every day that life is sacred.

Dance in Beauty

INTRODUCTION

Sacred:
>*something that is honoured*
>*to do with the purpose and intent we bring to our actions*
>*relating at a level of feeling, a place of authenticity, integrity*
>*and vulnerability;*
>*connecting with others and a greater goal*
>*a place beyond limits, after fear has been overcome*
>*in harmony with all life; balanced*

———

We live in a world where it is, apparently, easy to be happy – all we have to do is buy the right car, the smartest clothing and the most revitalizing shampoo. Our conditioning teaches us to look for and expect happiness outside ourselves – in a good job, a good salary, a good house, a family. Since everybody else follows the conditioning, it's easy for us to do so too. However, external symbols of happiness may satisfy the ego but they do not heal the soul. We need to listen to ourselves rather than the din of social expectation.

You, like many people in our age, may have a deep, niggling feeling of doubt, confusion or unhappiness as you strive for (or even achieve) your goals. That is your soul calling out to you to turn inward and work on changing yourself. Accepting that you are worth the effort is a sacred choice. You honor yourself to make it.

This book is a story about what happened to someone who made the choice.

Sacred Business is, therefore, about an individual and how he attempted to take on a more inclusive, creative, and responsible way of living. It describes a bridging from one world to another – an almost entirely different world represented in the character of Heather Campbell. This may be the story of Bill and Heather, but we believe that all such journeys of awakening are similar in direction if not detail. We hope that in Bill's experiences, thoughts, and in his reactions to

Heather's words, you will find something that speaks to your own personal situation.

We hope too that this book speaks at a macro level – to a business world attempting to wake up to the realities of ethics, environmental impact, vision, community, values, learning, and change. The teachings in this book address each of those issues and more. How open business is to them is part of the story.

We see no conflict between the aims of a sacred life and the demands of a profitable business. We believe the concerns of modern organizations are very similar to the challenges of living in a sacred manner: how do we use our time effectively, how do we tolerate complexity and ambiguity, how do we adapt flexibly to change, how do we make principle-based decisions, how can we understand and be understood, how can we prevent making the same mistakes over and over again?

The answers are to be found in the power and value of simplicity, in the crucial need for balance, in the empowerment gained from having multiple perceptions, and in the difference between, and equal importance of, active manifestation (masculine, yang) and receptive creativity (feminine, yin). Perhaps, in time, this understanding may lead to organizations that are more open to nurturing all our aspects – the emotions, the body, and the spirit as well as the mind. Organizations fit for business and the soul – those that nurture our need for self-development as well as our need for cash.

But this is not a how-to book, or a book of strategies or implementation plans. The sacred organizations we imagine, with their different emphasis on what's important, will only be created when individuals rediscover their own new priorities and make them real in their lives. Sacred companies will be created from the inside out. Business, like everything in life, is a reflection of ourselves.

Many of the teachings in this book are based on ancient, indigenous, earth-based wisdom and the peoples who 'carry' it. By observing the patterns and rhythms of nature, these people saw a model of harmony, flux, and balance which they were able to integrate into their own personal lives and communities. The knowledge of how to do this is not a collection of data separated from action. It is accessed through ceremony, creativity, reflection, and dialogue: in other words, through living it. This (literally) vital knowledge balances the wholeness of the individual with the oneness of the whole.

Why should this information be so valuable today? Because the history of business has been the history of division rather than inclusiveness. We have long emphasized the head-based skills of separation: logic, analysis, control, and measurement. It was these very same skills that gave us the industrial and technological revolutions and with them the power to manipulate our physical environment. We have transmuted that desire to manipulate into our relationships with others, characterized as they are by our struggles for power and dominion. And, seemingly encouraged by our success in bringing ourselves material comfort, we have internalized this urge to separate, placing our faith in the rational and scientific, and fearing to trust the messages from our own emotions, bodies, and spirit.

This multi-leveled drive towards separation has brought environmental crises to our outer world and psychological and spiritual crises in our inner worlds. There are strong signs now that we are waking up to these outcomes and beginning to understand that it was we who caused them through the choices we made. We have forgotten our place in the undifferentiated web of life which connects us to nature, each other, and ourselves. It is time to put ourselves back together again – to re-member.

Uniting in a whole that incorporates our wonderful diversity will help us learn, grow and do better business, without the stresses, tension, and imbalance that living in detachment brings.

First, however, we need to re-member how to be whole ourselves.

The SOUTH:
PLACE *of* EMOTIONS,
TRUST *and*
INNOCENCE

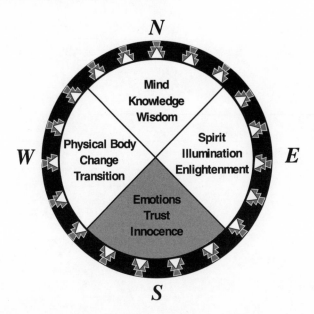

The journey to wholeness requires that you look honestly, openly and with courage into yourself, into the dynamics that lie behind what you feel, what you perceive, what you value and how you act. It is a journey through your defences and beyond so that you can experience consciously the nature of your personality, face what it has produced in your life, and choose to change that.

Gary Zukav, The Seat of the Soul

The membership of the Institute of Directors in Pall Mall, London comprises some of the most powerful, experienced, successful, traditional, serious, dull, staid, old-fashioned and pompous business people in the whole of Great Britain; and, before I met Heather, I desperately wanted to be one of them.

In fact, my friend and colleague Paul already was a member, and it was as his guest that I entered that esteemed institution one bright and sunny July afternoon. The morning-coated concierge opened the door for us just as we reached the top step, greeted us in the clipped, perfunctory manner that passes for civility in the best clubs and ushered us over to the receptionist, who took Paul's membership number and inquired the nature of our business. Such formality, such a sense of custom and order – this, I felt, was what a professional businessman should aspire to.

We were at the IOD to meet Heather Campbell, a consultant, known at that time to neither of us, but who was, in effect, a friend of a friend of a friend. Paul and I were partners in one of the large, international consultancies, jointly responsible for the change practice. We were in search of help and advice, because we knew that things were changing in the world of business, and we knew equally well that we needed to change the structure and behaviors of our team mates if we were to survive in a harshly competitive environment. Like most consultants, we always found it easier to fix other people's problems more than our own, so there was no sense of irony in a change consultancy casting about for a change consultant. Nobody we had interviewed to date, however, had quite met our objective of finding someone both capable *and* interesting. Heather was about to end our search. What I didn't appreciate at the time was that she was also about to begin another one.

I remember once a scene in a nature documentary which showed a clearing full of animals gradually sensing that a lion was about to enter the vicinity. One by one the creatures stopped their feeding and scratching and stood frozen, sniffing in heightened anticipation in the direction of the still-invisible predator. Heather's entrance was similar. Paul and I were sitting at a table in that huge room of wood panels and leather chairs, chatting about business but mostly simply enjoying soaking up the atmosphere. The first indications that something unusual was happening was the rustling of newspapers, as first one member, then another and then still another noticed that the latest guest to have been escorted into the Director's room was dressed not in dark suit and sober tie but in a small jacket and white dress which reached barely half way down the thigh. Not smartly trimmed hair, but long, highlighted curls. Not a watch of impeccable Swiss craftsmanship, but a turquoise necklace, depicting a bird of prey with its wings outstretched.

Heather had arrived and Paul and I were astonished, but then we were not alone in having that response. Paul leapt immediately up to greet her, arm outstretched, and for a minute I thought he was going to throw his jacket around her to protect her modesty. But Paul was a master performer.

'Heather!' he said. 'I'm Paul Chambers. Thank you for coming.'

'A pleasure, Paul. Hi.'

Heather smiled warmly and then glanced down at me as I sat at the table. It was only then that I realized that Paul had not bothered to introduce me. Flustered, I got up.

'Hello,' I said.

'You must be Bill?'

'Yes, I am,' I replied. 'Please, let's sit.'

I ordered tea, and as newspapers returned to reading height all around the room, the three of us began our meeting.

————

Heather Campbell had been born in Scotland to a Jewish family who owned a whisky distillery. The combination of these three facts already made her more interesting than most of the consultants we knew, but her later life was even more remarkable. After several years of study culminating in a degree in cultural anthropology from Brown University, Rhode Island, she had developed a fascination for Native American tradition and teachings and had, after a series of unusual events, spent seven years of her life studying with an organization called the Deer Tribe. The Deer Tribe was committed to the self-development of its members, and used a fusion of modern psychology and shamanic ritual and ceremony to that end. But, as I sat that July afternoon in the confines of the Institute of Directors, I understood nothing of what she described. To be honest, I found it difficult to concentrate, because all I could think about was the white dress and the turquoise owl, and how this was such an embarrassing situation in such an important place. The mantra 'first impressions, first impressions' was going through my head and I wondered how we could employ anyone who was so seemingly insensitive to the implicit rules of business. Paul had apparently put such thoughts to one side, and he questioned Heather, in his typically bullish manner, about what she had done and what she thought she could do for us. I remember thinking: 'this woman is from another world and this is never going to work.' I couldn't imagine how she could ever change herself enough to be suitable and effective in business.

———

After the meeting, Paul and I shared a taxi back to the office.

'So, what did you think?' asked Paul. He was testing me, as usual. It was a habit of his that really annoyed me, since I often thought he was buying time, leaving himself in a position to belittle my own opinions if he felt it left his sounding better. For partners, we had a strangely combative way of communicating.

'Well, um, she's certainly different ...' I ventured.

'But *what* was she wearing?' said Paul, scowling. 'Really! She'll have to smarten up!'

'Yes. Did you see that chap next to us staring at her legs?'

We both laughed. The taxi edged its away around Trafalgar Square and back towards the city.

'I liked all that stuff about warriors, though,' said Paul. 'There're a few of our guys who could do with a kick up the arse. Put them all through warrior training, make them a bit more tough, get them to think for themselves for a change. Then we won't have to do so much! "Warrior", yes, I like that. But we'll have to get her to tone most of her language down. Medicine Women. Medicine Wheels. Pipe ceremonies. I don't think she realizes that this is the business world, not Glastonbury.'

'So, do you think we'll use her?' I asked. It seemed Paul had already made up his mind.

'Oh, I think that we probably will. It's good to do something a bit different. And if we like the warrior thing, maybe we can get her in to do it for our clients as one of our offerings. Let's get her in at our place a couple of times; put her through her paces; see what she knows.'

We met Heather at our offices in the City of London several times over the next couple of months, but my memories of those meetings are vague. I do know that they followed a similar pattern every time – we would talk, and talk, and talk at Heather, explaining this model, describing that approach, and Heather in turn would listen, politely and patiently. It was strange. I think our attitude at first was that we were auditioning Heather; but I'd been in theater years before and I knew that auditions generally focused around encouraging the candidate to display their talents, rather than the director using up the whole half hour describing what a brilliant production it was going to be.

Why did we feel the need to say so much? Nerves, perhaps? I had a friend who found it difficult to be comfortable when meeting new people, partly because he was the one who created the discomfort. He was so nervous when faced with a stranger at a party, for example, that he would launch into long, one-sided conversations, ostensibly to express how at ease he was. Terrified of silences, since he felt those were the moments when the listeners would think how bored they were, my friend would plough straight on without pause or abeyance. He left his prey exhausted and irritable, and he could see that; which rather supported his belief that he was a person who found it difficult to make friends.

But why would we be nervous with Heather? We were the ones in control, we were the ones offering the work. We were highly successful businessmen; what had we to fear from this woman?

Perhaps it wasn't nerves then. What else could be causing these meetings to be so unbalanced? Was Heather nervous? Possibly, though I neglected to ask her.

So, despite all the talk, the three of us seemed to be missing some point of connection: we didn't appear to be bridging the gap. I think this was partly because Heather didn't seem to be enthused by any of the things we told her. On one occasion, Paul introduced her to one of the latest and most acclaimed theories that had just come on to the consultant scene: punctuated equilibrium. It was about change. It states that revolutionary change occurs in bursts of increasing speed – the periods of calmer, incremental change getting shorter and shorter as time progresses, with each period of revolutionary change appearing to be more extreme than the last. I remember the definition clearly, but I remember the image better. If you were to represent the progression of punctuated equilibrium on a graph, you'd get what appeared to be an aggressive stroke of lightning going across the page, or a wild line on a heart monitor.

Paul proudly drew the graph on the flip chart and explained the idea behind it. As far as we were concerned at the time, this was as good as it got – as insightful and modern a perception of the nature of change as we could expect.

But Heather's response was typically enigmatic. For the first time since we'd been holding these meetings, she stood up and took the marker pen from Paul, and said:

'So what? It doesn't tell us anything we don't already know. Does it solve? Does it give us a miracle cure for slowing things down?'

'No,' I replied, angry at her stubbornness, 'but we can infer from it how people need to be in organizations in continuous change. They need to be flexible, rule-breaking, tolerant of ambiguity.' I was sounding like a consultant.

'And are they?' asked Heather.

'Not as often as they should be,' I confessed. 'But then again, that's our job, isn't it – to help them get that way?'

'But your jagged line isn't going to help them. Why is it always lines with you consultants, anyway – graphs, two-by-twos, the bottom line? Look!'

Heather, impassioned, strode over to the window and gestured outside.

'Nature couldn't survive if it were rigid and linear. She is innately flexible and adaptable.

'Beneath the din of man-made hustle and bustle, there's a different rhythm – the rise and fall of the sun, the wax and wane of the moon, the cycle of the seasons. Nature can teach us to welcome change rather than be stressed by it. Change is both inevitable and necessary. That's how new growth happens, whether in a garden or a company. We must learn to listen to the voices normally drowned out by our left-brain chatter.'

As she talked, she flowed across the room and back.

'The business world must start to move its collective body, connect to its heart and passion and reawaken to its ability to feel. And you're definitely going to have to stop talking so much and start *doing* more!' she said emphatically.

When I look back on that moment, I think of it as the first, faint sign of my awakening, because I became aware that I had two voices in my head. They were both me, but they were saying two very different things.

The first voice was the one I was most used to – dismissive, cynical, maybe a little defensive. It told me that Heather had blown it, that she had shown herself to be hopelessly naive. I was a graduate of English Literature, so I knew all about the poetry of trees and animals. Wordsworth and daffodils, Shelley and skylarks – I had studied how enchanting nature could be. But that was then, and this was now. Any business person worth his salt would laugh Heather out of court if she tried to suggest that the rhythms of nature in any way connected to the pressures and stresses of late twentieth-century business. She was being overly simplistic in dismissing our change graph so completely.

But then there was another voice, albeit a faint one, that gently suggested that there was something in what she said that was worth consideration. And deep inside me I knew why that voice was speaking: it was because Heather was patently *not* stupid, *not* naive. What was most disabling at that moment was a niggling sensation (which seemed madness even to admit to myself), that, far from Heather being the one who had missed the point, it was *we*, and most of the business world with us, that was failing to understand.

Then, in an instant, I realized why our meetings had been so unbalanced, why they had been characterized by our long, detailed presentations coupled with Heather's patient listening. We were behaving in a profoundly typical way, the way business had always encouraged us to behave. We were the ones with the knowledge – the big challenge was to make sure that everyone else understood it. That was the central tenet behind our consultancy: Me Expert, You Not. It was how we were with our clients. The clients were the people who might mess up our beautiful methodology and our track record, but as long as we kept on getting them to understand us and conform to our view of the world, who knows, they might not screw up that badly.

Our impulse as businessmen was towards being understood. It made us certain, predictable, closed. Understanding something new – and all that implied about having to be open, vulnerable and unsure – was not an experience we allowed ourselves to undergo very often at all. How would we let anything new into our lives, if we couldn't let go of what we already knew?

I was intrigued – not, at that point by Heather's words, but by this dialog inside my head; by this sense that in some intuitive way, Heather and I had made a connection, even though the largest part of me was dismissing these 'insights' as idiotic. Did I understand yet? No. Yet old certainties had been dislodged. There was space where before there had been a sealed door. Something had been set in motion. Somewhere, perhaps, between man-made complexity and nature's simplicity, between the straight line and the circle, was a more comprehensive vision of life.

It was Paul who snapped me out of my reverie. It was if he was speaking for my logical, left brain self.

'Look, Heather, our colleagues and our clients are professionals in some very senior positions. They are not going to be convinced by all this talk of the seasons and stars. They're very clever people.'

I could see that that last remark had annoyed Heather.

'I didn't mention stars!' she said, pointedly.

'Look, let's call it a day for today,' said Paul, hurrying on. 'I've got another meeting at four. Why don't you and Bill go ahead and book the next meeting.'

As he reached the door, he turned back.

'Oh and one more thing, Heather. I've been meaning to say. The clothes you wore at the IOD that first day we met?' he paused, as if looking for the right words. 'They're, well, right out. OK? Can you wear something a bit, er, *longer* next time?'

'Congratulations for finally getting up the courage to say something, Paul,' replied Heather. 'I'm sorry if my suit shocked you. As you know, I've been in Los Angeles making radio and TV programs for the last few years. I realize that my attire was more suited to the Californian business world than a meeting at the IOD.' She paused '...Although, my suit probably did cost more than yours and Bill's put together.'

'Yes, well ...' muttered Paul. I suppressed a smile.

'And, as I'd never been to the IOD before, I had no idea what to expect.'

Paul shot a look at Heather. 'Anyway, I'll leave you to it. See you later, Heather.' He nodded across the room to me. 'Bill.'

Heather and I were left alone in the room. She picked her briefcase up and took from it a small, black diary.

'So you do make some concessions to straight British business then, Heather?' I teased, gesturing at her case, though even that was covered in wood veneer and not the normal leather.

'I think it's beautiful,' replied Heather, not joking. 'And I thought you'd have realized by now that I'd prefer something made out of a tree.'

It was comments like that which made me more and more convinced of Heather. She was good-humored and she knew when to be self-deprecatory. But most of all, she knew herself. We were still a million miles away from each other in terms of how we saw the world, but I knew, beyond doubt, that she was genuine. But what do I mean by genuine? Did it matter to me then how sincere and earnest she was about her beliefs, how quietly convinced she was that she was right? It didn't matter at all if she was crazy, or so far from the 'normal' world that she had nothing to say to it. What did matter was that this was a risky relationship I might be entering into. I had my standing in the organization to think about, let alone what my friends and family might think. Part of me told me very strongly to proceed with caution before we committed to Heather and used her in our organization. Another much quieter and, at that time, much weaker part of me told me a profound connection had already been made at a level other than business.

'Why don't we have the next meeting at my house, Bill? I've traveled into the center a few times now – it must be your turn to return the favor.'

'Well, we're both very busy,' I answered, gathering papers off the table, 'and you're in, where was it ...?'

'Surbiton.'

'Surbiton, that's right.' Where the heck was Surbiton? I wasn't even convinced it was a real place. All I could associate with Surbiton was a TV sitcom set in a part of London's suburban sprawl. 'So you see, we're both very busy and it's difficult to squeeze in travel time ...'

'Don't worry,' she interrupted, making a waving gesture. 'The things I was going to invite you to are both in the evening.'

'Oh, so you mean social events,' I said. I couldn't begin to imagine what Heather, the Medicine Woman from suburbia, might do for a social life.

'Oh no,' Heather said. 'It's work. I work better in the evenings.'

I didn't ask why.

'I've got a medicine group next Tuesday and I'm giving a talk in Piccadilly later in the month. You both should come. It's time you saw me in action. All you've really seen me do so far is listen, although I am pretty good at that.'

I smiled. Medicine group?

'OK, Heather, let's do it,' I said, nodding. 'I'll check with Paul and give you a call to confirm.'

We started to get ready to leave, making final checks that we'd collected everything together.

As we shook hands, I said what was on my mind.

'Erm, Heather. What should I bring to a medicine group?'

'Just you,' she said, with a smile. 'And a paper and pen if you want to take notes. I'll provide everything else.'

I paid the cab driver as Paul took our coats and bags from the car. From the outside, Heather's house appeared to be a normal semi-detached in a quiet avenue of apparently identical houses. We walked down the short, curving driveway overhung and protected from view by a large Cherry Laurel tree. On the black door there was a sign, one of those pottery door hangings often used to denote the Bathroom or Someone's Room. This one said: *Here lives an owl lover.* Heavy curtains were drawn in the huge, arched window to our right, but Paul pointed at three objects hanging in a mobile from the curtain rail: crystals. 'Uh oh,' we said in unison.

We rang the bell and a smiling Heather answered, pulling open the door and gesturing us inside – she was already in conversation with some other people inside. We walked in. The first thing we were aware of was the size of the room – at some stage much of the first floor had been removed so that the lounge area's ceiling was in fact the roof of the house. It was like a huge vaulted baronial hall – stone fireplace off to the right, open wooden staircase sweeping up to the rooms above. The second thing we noticed were the decorations on every surface or shelf or hanging from the walls – an enormous collection of tribal masks, statues, paintings, carvings, sculptures and elaborate caskets from different religions and belief systems around the world. Animal skins were draped over chairs. On the mantle piece were two skulls, one animal, the other definitely human – though embossed and beaded and finished with two staring silver eyes. Evidently, Heather had taken her cultural anthropology very seriously. And, as we glanced around the room, we saw a menagerie of stuffed animals – a hawk here, an owl up there, a beaver and an armadillo and a toad; and there in the fireplace, a snake curled around the branch of a tree. Nature, worldly and other worldly, was in this room.

I looked at Paul and tried to figure out what he was thinking. I was contemplating how this room changed my previous expectations of Heather, if at all. I was trying to categorize her, and the only box big enough seemed to be eccentric – I just didn't know whether she was going to turn out to be a harmless one. Certainly, no-one I knew, no-one I had ever known, owned a house like this. So how big, or how small, did that make my world?

I noticed that Paul had moved into the kitchen to talk with Heather – I reckoned that was a good idea given that we knew nobody else in the place and I had no sense of what I might say to any of them. I was reassured to an extent, since none of the ten or so attendees looked in any way odd and in fact looked satisfyingly ordinary. But who were they? What were they here for? What was going to happen? I realized, as Heather came out of the kitchen and began to call a start to the meeting, that I was utterly disorientated. There was nothing here that was within my comfort zone.

Following Heather's invitation, we gathered round a large, low coffee table of dark, carved wood, and formed a circle as best we could, some sitting on sofas and chairs, others sitting cross-legged or kneeling.

'Let's begin shall we?' she said. 'We have some newcomers here tonight as well as the regulars. Welcome to everybody both new and old. Let's start with everybody introducing themselves. Tell us your name and a little bit about who you are and what you do.'

Heather nodded at the person to her left, inviting her to begin.

I listened with interest – was there some pattern here to who these people were? Had they all done similar things? What bound them together? But there was no clue. There was a record producer and his girlfriend. There was a middle age housewife from 'just two streets away' and a sixteen-year-old girl, who turned out to be South West England's Junior tennis champion. There was an elderly man who was something in the civil service. A friend of the record producer's, who designed and made clothes for a living. There were others of similarly diverse backgrounds and there was Paul and there was me. The only thing that we seemed to have in common was that we were all here to listen to Heather.

Heather began to lay out objects around a circle.

'This evening,' she told us, 'I'm going to be telling you about the Star Maiden's Circle – a self-development tool from the Deer Tribe which shows you how to decipher the encoding which causes you to repeat negative patterns in your lives. It also shows you how you choreograph the energy in your life – and whether your design is pain- or pleasure-based. The path of pain is called the Circle of Foxes – imagine the fox with its tail in its mouth, always running around and around. The path of pleasure is known as the Star Maiden's Circle.

'"Why is it a circle?", I hear you ask. Well, the Native Americans comprised of hundreds of different peoples speaking a multitude of languages and living in a vast expanse of land. They disagreed about many things, but all honored the sacred hoop. The Christians have the cross, the Jews the Star of David – the Native Americans, like most ancient peoples who lived in nature, chose the circle. The Sun, the Moon and the stars are all round. The rhythm of nature is cyclical: look at the seasons or the Buddhist belief in reincarnation – birth, life, death, rebirth, life and so on.

'The circle is representative of Everything – the All – and Nothing – the Void. It is the symbol of perfect balance and harmony within a universe where all forms of all things are interconnected. Einstein got it right.

'Like most of the wheels of information I use, this circle has eight points – the four cardinals and the four non-cardinals. At each point, I place an object as a symbol. Let me introduce each one and describe its significance, since each point on the compass has an individual power. Each point allows us an insight into a particular part of our lives.'

As she visited each place, starting at the bottom of the circle and working clockwise, she touched each object gently and lifted it for us to see. As I look back on it now, I realize that my attention was particularly drawn to Heather's description of the four non-cardinals points of the circle.

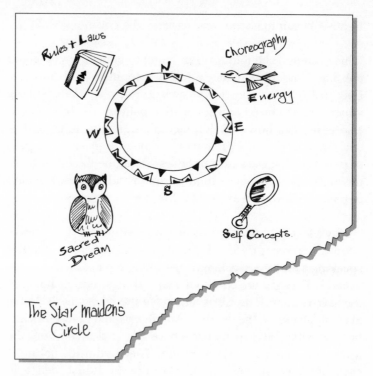

Heather said:

'In the South West, we have a turquoise stone and a wooden owl representing your dream and symbols of life experience. If you are working in the dark of this place you will be doing what we call *walking asleep*. You'll have no sacred dream, no awareness of why you came into this lifetime and what you are here to do. You will be living the dream of others – doing what you think others expect of you. One of the questions to ask yourself in this direction is: What is your sacred dream, what is it you do best which is your gift to others?

'In the North West, we have an indigo stone and a bible representing human rules and laws. In the dark side of this place, you are trapped by the need to obey moral, social, political, civil and religious laws as opposed to Sacred Law. Honoring the former instead of the latter keeps you in negative behavioral patterns. In this direction it is appropriate to ask: What are the teachings you are here to learn?

'In the North East, a green stone and a hummingbird representing impeccable choreography of energy. If you are working in the dark of this place, you'll waste time and energy, you'll be involved in procrastination, self-sabotage, laziness or self-pity. What are your priorities in organizing your life? Do you come first or last? Is your choreography of energy based on the law of maximum efficiency, minimum effort – or vice versa?

'And in the South East we have an orange stone and a small mirror representing your concepts of self. You carry these self-concepts with you all the time; however, they do shift as you begin to discover yourself through self-development. How do you see yourself – in flattering or derogatory terms?'

I remember thinking two things as I heard this list of objects, symbology and questions. First, that this was all way beyond anything I'd heard before. Was this sacred native religion? Was this hippy mumbo jumbo masquerading as pop psychology? To be honest, I had no knowledge or experience of either of those areas of activity, but I'd have felt happier then to have been able to make a safe and dismissive pigeon hole of whatever it was I didn't understand. I was uncomfortable and I wanted to make a joke of it; or simply assume that what little I knew was automatically superior to anyone else's beliefs. I was anxious largely because of the second thought I had that evening: that this litany of beliefs had a power and sense that I could not, in fact, dismiss out of hand. The objects and symbols meant nothing to me, but the questions were different. Those questions were for me.

Heather lit the candle.

'Lighting the candle ignites the circle. It's the sign that we are beginning the Medicine Wheel.'

———

Later, as the meeting broke up and people fell into conversation, I moved across the room to ask Paul what he thought. He looked stern. 'Hmm; very interesting,' he said. I wasn't convinced that he was telling the truth. 'And you?'

What *did* I think? I couldn't let Paul know that the Star Maiden's questions were beginning to gnaw at my conscience: he'd think I was a fool. There were some elements of the evening that made me uncomfortable – the crystal skull, the symbols and the colored stones all seemed silly and unrealistic. This I could share with Paul, because I know that's what we were good at: ridiculing other points of view. But Paul was really asking my opinion on a business level rather than a personal one. *What has this strange circle of viewpoints and questions got to do with organizational change? What has Native American development tools, with all their ritual and mysticism, got to do with management consultancy?* I didn't know.

There was a deeper question too, one that in my mind seemed to come with a stronger voice and one which seemed more urgent to find the answer to. *What has the circle got to do with me?*

As others were leaving, Paul and I decided to go too. We felt no more able to make conversation now than we did when we first arrived.

We moved across to Heather.

'So, Paul, Bill. What did you think? Did you find it interesting?'

Paul spoke first.

'Heather – it certainly gave us lots to think about!' he said. A nothing answer, although I didn't know what I might have said.

'There's one thing, though, Heather,' I interjected. An idea for a question had just popped into my head, to my relief. 'I'm still no clearer as to what a medicine group actually is. I didn't see any medicine being given out tonight.'

Heather said: 'Not in the sense that a pharmacist might dispense your prescription in a little bottle of tablets, no. In the West, medicine is about consumption, it's something you take – and it's usually pretty nasty stuff. On my path, medicine is something you gain or learn from your experiences. There's good medicine and there's bad medicine. Good medicine is anything that restores you to balance and wholeness – so it can be the sight of a beautiful tree, a refreshing glass of water, a meeting with a friend, a story, an understanding about something. Bad medicine is anything that speaks to you in a darker way. So if I had three flat tyres on the way to a meeting with you, my Native American companions would say "oh, that's bad medicine, very *bad* medicine".' She laughed.

'Western medicine is about curing illness rather than enhancing health. We talk about an apple a day keeping the doctor away, but that's not what is practiced. In general we only deal with our health when we get ill.'

From nowhere, a cat had leapt up on to Heather's lap and she began to stroke its head. 'For the Native Americans, a beautiful sunrise was probably the equivalent of the daily apple. Yes, the people here tonight have their fair share of ailments, but what they are looking for is medicine that enhances and improves their lives. This medicine is something that can give them power over their lives through learning about themselves. This is medicine for inner growth.'

I thought of our company and the thousands like them, who read the literature of team building and culture and leadership and build up huge tracts of information on 'best practice'. But do we use it? There's a part of us that knows instinctively what's right and what's wrong, what's good and what's less good; but time and again, tragically and consistently, we wait for the pain to get unavoidable before we look to fix things. We wait for our teams and cultures and leaders to get unbearable before we do anything. I thought of my career in consultancy to date, and how I only worked with clients who were trying to rescue themselves, to stop the pain. We didn't make our money from healthy organizations trying to be healthier. I felt like a fox in that Circle of Foxes.

Unclear as my intuition was at first, I knew there was something important here about the difference between making it better, and making it better ...

Three days later, I sat in a meeting in our offices, hearing the drone of report after report being read out. As was my habit, I was doodling, and, over the long hours of this meeting, I had created a work of scribbles and jottings that was either akin to the Sistine Chapel or the hallucinogenic ramblings of a stoned cartoonist. Swirls and loops of black ink provided ornate, page-high frames for frames that were themselves inside frames; geometric shapes copied each other again and again, mirroring themselves back into the deep perspectives of the paper. Was this the only outcome of that mind mapping class I'd attended?, I wondered.

I turned a snigger into a cough for the benefit of my fellow attendees and made a show of getting my handkerchief out to blow my nose. The report-reader-in-waiting watched me to check that I was not going to interrupt again, and then returned to his task. I returned to mine.

At the center of my ornate page were words and not drawings. They were in the form of four questions, those that had been with me since I'd first heard them at Heather's medicine group:

My answers lacked conviction, or were in the form of other questions. Why sacred? I'm not religious. What's sacred got to do with me? What teachings? I hadn't realized I was here to learn. Wasn't learning just an optional byproduct of experience rather than the core purpose of life?

Priorities? Hah! Now this was an easier one. My priorities were clear. I'd once been on a course where they'd asked us to list our passions. We'd all put family at the top of the list. What would we do with an extra four hours in the day, they'd asked. Easy, we'd responded; we'd spend it with our children. Even those who didn't have children were putting that down. So identifying priorities was not the problem. What was a challenge was actually putting them first. But, as everyone on the course agreed, that's life. *C'est la guerre.* You've got to work, haven't you? Important to give the family a good standard of living. Good education for the children. Maybe do well enough to retire early – *then* we can spend more time with the kids.

Did we believe ourselves in saying all this? Yes, unfortunately, we did.

I could already see a future for myself where I would fall into exactly the same trap, a future characterized by that same gap between saying and doing. Is that how I thought about myself then – as a hypocrite? No, too strong a word. A cheat? I certainly didn't cheat the organization. They had the best of my attention and effort. So was I cheating myself? I'd never thought of it that way. As I stared at the page wondering how I could answer that question, my eyes flicked repeatedly back to question one, as if the questions were linked and cumulative rather than distinct and independent.

I felt I was on the edge of even bigger, potentially uncomfortable questions about my life and my place in it. It was to my relief, then, that someone called a break in the meeting, and we all made our way to the coffee machine to talk about last night's TV.

***

After the evening of the Medicine Wheel Group, we hadn't seen Heather for over a fortnight. The evening she'd invited us to at St James's was coming up, but another opportunity was to arise first.

From my office high up over the City, I looked out over London. The maze of London streets beneath me carried streams of people back and forth, but there seemed to be nothing of the circle here. And the only wheels in sight ground out slowly the constant rush hour of city life. I watched a cycle courier weaving between the stationary traffic.

My PC beeped. An e-mail. Another e-mail. Without turning my chair, I reached over and hit the Return button, and watched the message expand on to the screen. It was from Paul.

Reference: IOD dinner.
Let's invite Heather. Introduce her to friends and colleagues. See what
they make of her.
Let me know what you think. – P.

We were hosting a dinner meeting at the IOD to discuss some pertinent questions of the day with various associates, from our company and others that we either once did work with, or hoped at some point to work with in the future.

I thought of Heather's previous visit to the Institute, and, smiling, sent an immediate reply to Paul.

Perhaps I was both disappointed and relieved when Heather arrived in a modest black cocktail dress. It was an entirely appropriate match for our other guests' black tie and tuxedos. In fact the whole evening went without incident, except for a moment near the beginning when we introduced Heather to our associates.

'And this is Heather,' said Paul. 'Heather's going to be working with us over the coming months on some change issues we're facing. Heather's a medicine woman.'

There was some general, embarrassed shuffling. 'Ah,' said one of our guests.

I expected the description to cause a stir amongst the gin and tonics and olives, but it was only afterwards, when our guests had left and the three of us sat together in the lounge, that we realized how annoyed Heather herself was.

'I'm not just annoyed, I'm pissed off.' She pulled her cigarettes from her bag and took one from the packet, holding it like a pointer in her right hand. 'You've no idea how long I spent finding the most appropriate clothing tonight – and I mean hours in front of the mirror – trying something on, looking in the mirror, trying something on, looking in the mirror ... And then you go and introduce me as medicine woman! I might as well have brought my drum and and worn feathers in my hair. And that's exactly what they saw when you introduced me with those words.'

'But you are a medicine woman,' I complained. Why was she being so difficult?

'Yes I know I am,' she said, with a slow, exaggerated nod of her head. 'But if I appear like one, people will instantly go into judgment and have a preconceived notion about who I am and what I can do. God, how many business men wouldn't change channels if a medicine woman came on TV tonight?'

'Yes, but isn't it more truthful to be who you are?' I asked, genuinely not understanding what we'd done to offend. As far as we were concerned, we were proud to have a medicine woman working with us. It made us different.

'Forget about who I am,' said Heather, shaking the cigarette to dismiss my suggestion. 'I am a medicine woman – I can also be a business consultant. Remember, you asked me to wear the mask – and I have no problem with that. But we have to decide on one story and all keep to it.'

'I thought that people like you were supposed to be more honest than the rest of us,' Paul's sarcastic comment hit the conversation like a brick. 'Don't you think it's deceitful to disguise yourself?'

Heather shot a glance at him. 'Why do you think there's anything deceitful in wearing a mask – all that matters is that you know when to take it off. Business people have put on what they think is the appropriate mask and it's become super-glued to their face. They've become the mask; everything they do is for the persona of the mask rather than for the real person behind it.' She continued to stare at Paul, waiting for him to respond.

I listened intently to what was being said.

'Well,' he began, raising a hand in the direction of the bar and nodding at the waiter 'what you wore tonight was fine.'

'Oh I see! Really Paul, you're being such a hypocrite,' Heather shook her head, laughing to herself in exasperation. She lit her cigarette and blew smoke up to the ceiling. 'You didn't want me to be a sexy woman but you don't mind me being weird. If you're going to introduce me as a medicine woman, I'll dress like a medicine woman, because that's what people will see no matter how smartly I'm dressed. If you introduce me as a consultant, I'll look like a consultant. Which do you want?'

Paul considered his answer for a moment, but Heather didn't give him a chance to reply.

'Anyway, it's not just about how I look. It's about what a mode of dress implies about my knowledge in certain areas. Sexy women and medicine women aren't assumed to know anything about business.'

'Oh, come on, Heather; let's be realistic about this ...'

I'm sure I saw Heather mutter something under her breath.

'... You can't know as much about business as we do.'

'I don't pretend to, Paul,' she said, with forced politeness. 'But neither can you be expected to know about self-development and balance in people. That's why I'm stepping into the business world now – because of that specific lack of knowledge and the problems it's causing.'

'Go on.' Paul gestured at her to continue.

'OK,' Heather sat forward. 'What's the main theme in all those books and reports you gave me to demonstrate what business is most preoccupied with at the moment?'

It didn't need much thinking about.

'People,' Paul said.

'Getting the best out of your people!' I added, quoting a seminar of ours.

'Our people are our greatest asset!' echoed Paul. 'The biggest cliché of the day.'

'Exactly,' nodded Heather. 'All of a sudden the business world has woken up: it's all about people, all about maximizing their potential. The problem is there's little genuine understanding in business of what people are, why they do what they do and what they want from life. Traditional training focuses on the tools people use rather than who they are.'

'So where should we be focusing ...?' asked Paul brusquely.

'On the lack of balance and self-responsibility in people,' replied Heather.

The waiter appeared at our table and took an order for one more round of drinks.

'Change in organizations happens from the outside in,' Heather continued. 'Which is absolutely the wrong way round.'

'But things are improving,' I argued. 'We're doing away with huge hierarchies, which has got to be better for people.'

'But that's just more of the same process,' said Heather. 'You're just externalizing the change you want. If a company flattens its hierarchy; or if it does away with offices and goes open plan, what's it looking for?'

'Synergy through teamwork,' I offered. 'Greater creativity, trust, openness – all that sort of stuff.'

'Fine!' Heather carried on, sitting forward in her chair. 'But the point is that a flat organization *implies* that it wants trust and those other things, but it doesn't *supply* them in itself. In effect, all you're doing is rearranging the building blocks – you're not changing the blocks themselves.'

Heather pushed three beer mats round the surface of the coffee table to show us what she meant. It looked a little like she was doing the 'pea under the cup' trick.

'The qualities you list are only unleashed when people know themselves, know what they really want and then make the appropriate changes to their attitudes and behaviors. If you want more open communication, people have to work on those parts of themselves that hold them back from being open. If you want trust, individuals have to remove the personal blocks and negative patterns that prevent them trusting and being trustworthy, and so on. That's creating change by working from the inside out.'

Heather picked up the three beer mats and put them together into a single pile.

'You understand organizations and their component parts – you know all about systems, structures and processes,' she said, sitting back in her chair with her glass of whiskey. 'I understand people.'

Then there was silence for a while. And suddenly, there was a great sense of relief in Paul and I. It was OK for Heather not to know about our work and for us not to know about Heather's.

And that's maybe why it could work out between us – we were diverse specialities offering a total solution. I could almost imagine the brochure we'd print up. The whole tone of the meeting changed.

'Actually,' Paul picked up the conversation cheerily, emptying the last of his brandy. 'We have a term for a way of thinking about companies, Heather – I wonder if it might be useful here?'

'Go on.'

'If we're helping a company rediscover its original purpose, we call it "green field" thinking,' he said, curling up his brow to show how serious he was. 'In other words, we say "If we could start this company all over again, before even the offices or factory had been built, what would we do differently and what would we do the same?" The point is that to think like that takes deliberate naiveté or ignorance. It's best to pretend you know nothing about business so that you can challenge even the most basic belief. Maybe you're there without having to pretend.'

'A green field. Oh I like that!' Heather said. She seemed genuinely excited by the metaphor. 'So, I'm a green field consultant?'

'Yes, I suppose you are ...' nodded Paul, looking across at me.

But Heather was not looking at either of us. She was forming a question in her imagination: 'If we could start again with only the green fields that were here before any of us, what would happen? How would we like it to be? What would we like to change about ourselves?'

'Do you really believe that business can be a place of balanced, self-responsible people?,' I asked Heather later, walking her back to the station. London's late night traffic buzzed and growled. 'Isn't it the work or the organization that constrains people? What happens about those people who hate their work? What can they do?'

'Well, first I'd ask them why they were bringing pain to themselves by putting their energy into something they claimed to hate,' she replied.

We paused to cross the road, passing a young girl sleeping in a shop doorway.

'And they can, like all of us, make work more meaningful in bringing focus and intent to what they do – they can strive everyday to do their tasks better. Or they can use their work to develop themselves – their ability to form relationships with their co-workers for example. There is always the potential to get more out of what we are doing.

'What about people who say things surrounded by people they don't like?'

'We all have the ability to change our perception. If I hate my colleagues and think my job's boring and that the boss is out to get me, only I have the power to look at the situation from a different angle. I don't need anyone else to change in that situation. Alternatively, I could change what I am looking at and redirect my focus. Even better, I could change my interpretations of my perceptions. Anyone can find something worthwhile in what they do.'

We approached the grand frontage of Charing Cross station, dodging taxis in the forecourt.

'Yes, yes,' I said impatiently, seeking to press Heather to a conculsion before we had to board our separate trains. 'But what about really *dull* jobs? Can an accountant be proud of a spreadsheet? Can a cleaner be proud of cleaning a toilet?'

'Only you can choose to care enough to make yourself proud,' she said, looking me directly in the eye. 'And if you can be proud of even your most mundane activities, then that pride has a chance of showing up in any other area of your life too.'

We waited under the departures board. A group of young businessmen fell by, looking crumpled and exhausted after a good night out. They munched happily on powerful smelling burgers, whose contents they struggled not to spill down their ties.

Heather smiled at the sight.

'If you want work to be meaningful, then you have to accept that it *isn't* always going to be fun,' she said. 'I think we can be more tolerant, even appreciative, of the mundane. To enjoy every minute of our work, to love everybody we work for, is a fantasy: we are doomed to failure and unhappiness to expect it. The dull, the mundane and the difficult, are parts of life which are just as valid as its flashes of joy and brilliance. Those are the bits that provide all the teaching.'

I remember very few of my dreams, but that night I recollected one vividly.

In my dream I was in my living room with my wife, Grace, watching TV. Our smoke alarm went off – a piercing scream. I tutted and held a cushion over my ears. Grace was shouting and running around the house, searching for the fire. I walked over to the smoke alarm and pulled out its battery. Then I went back to watching TV.

I remember very few of my dreams, and understand them even less.

At around this time I met a famous architect at a party. Emboldened by gin, I interrupted his discourse on where his work was taking him this year, and suddenly asked why business buildings aren't based on the circle. 'Why aren't there any round organizations?' I inquired, drawing the shape with my hands so that he understood what I meant.

His answer was clear and immediate. 'A round building would be a waste of space,' he explained, though not in a harsh way. 'All our furniture and equipment is square and you simply can't get as much of that stuff into a circle.'

'You can't get so many squares into a circle,' I heard someone else say, quietly.

I ignored the joke and the giggles it brought. I was building up for my own big line.

'It's a valid point you've made,' I said to the architect, prodding the air between us with a crisp for emphasis. 'As long as you have agreed to value *efficiency* above everything else.'

'Well yes!' he said, nodding. 'The priorities we live by create our lives.'

There was a silence.

'*That's* a good line,' I said, honestly.

'Ah yes,' he replied. 'I read it somewhere, in a book.'

I remember Heather once telling me that the Native Americans describe us as the sum of the dreaming of all our ancestors. The hopes our forefathers had, the things they feared, the mistakes they learned from and the successes they enjoyed, all these things contribute to what we experience today. The teaching also states that we stand as ancestors to tomorrow. We are the dreamers of the future.

This is why the Cherokee are raised with a sense of responsibility not just for today, but to the next seven generations. They are told to consider every decision they make in that light. Life is sacred, so living it needs care.

I wonder how such an attitude would affect modern business. Consider: what positive and negative outcomes from our actions today may ripple down the years and leave our successors in a heaven or hell not of their own making.

It is difficult to see this attitude of caring foresight being grasped with enthusiasm. Only a single generation ago, our forebears neglected to consider that the year 2000 needed explaining to the computers they were designing: 2000 does not equal 1900. It was a picky detail, one that they thought their sons and granddaughters would have the time and energy to attend to. Well, we have the energy, and the skill, but the time is running out. A lot of people are making a lot of money out of rectifying the situation now, of course, which proves that our actions have both negative and positive outcomes, depending on your point of view. Yet, the year 2000 issue stands as a symbol for our times, both monumental and banal, at once frightening and laughable, a testament to the dangers of not attending to the consequences of what we do. Elsewhere, the consequences of our pursuit of increased earnings per share have outcomes which are less banal and less laughable. Look at the impact on the environment and on indigenous peoples in the wider world, but also look closer to home, at the damage to social community and personal hope.

We must look at the benefits we gain from any change, but balance the benefits with the cost, and ask if it could have happened any other way.

I sat opposite the man in a bare white office. A clock ticked softly in the background.

I was carrying out a cultural audit of a medium-sized insurance company. Tony here – wiry frame, balding head, a single pen in his shirt pocket – was my fourth interview of the day and my thirtieth on this project overall.

I noticed Tony had long fingernails, like I imagined a guitarist's would be. But it was late in the day and I'd cut the preliminary chat to a minimum. I'd try and remember to ask him about his hobbies at the end.

I took Tony through the long list of questions on the sheets in front of me and made surreptitious notes on his body language. But this man had nothing to hide. He was clearly intent on telling me how he felt – and he did not feel good. With every question from me, he took a long pause before answering, staring out of the window as if carefully crafting his response. His answers were pretty much in alignment with everyone else I'd spoken to, but definitely more extremely expressed. He hated the new management, he hated the way they had treated him, he thought they were killing the company. As the questionnaire wore on, he grew redder and redder in the face, the pauses became longer, during which he swallowed hard as if to choke something back.

With some relief, I found I was at the general questions stage, the 'cool down' section. It was time to let Tony out of his misery.

I said: 'So Tony, is there anything else you'd like to tell me?'

A long pause, so extended that I looked out the window too to see if something had caught his eye. When I glanced back, Tony was shaking ever so slightly and swallowing again.

And then he began to cry.

I had never seen anyone cry in an office.

'Fifteen years,' he said. 'Fifteen years I've given to this company. They were *nothing*' – he spat the word out – 'when they started and they wanted me then didn't they? But this lot, they don't care who they harm. They chew you up and spit you out. They don't give a fuck. You're just meat here.'

He gazed out of the window and nodded to himself as much as to me. His lips were puffed up and wet with spittle.

'Meat,' he said again.

Just two weeks later I facilitated a session between the MD of a small design company and his sales team.

'I really want to hear your feedback about me,' Tom the MD said at one point. 'I can't tell you enough how important it is that I hear what you think of me. If I'm screwing up, I need to know. Or if I'm doing well, that would be nice to hear too.'

Silence.

'Honestly, there'll be no comeback. I don't care if it's really negative – if it's the truth, then I need to know. I won't sack anybody here for telling the truth.'

Silence again.

I intervened.

'Do you believe him?' I asked the team.

There was another silence, after which one of the team spoke up.

'Yeah,' she said, not moving from her slumped sitting position. Nothing more.

'Anyone else?' I asked.

Eventually, all six of the team nodded.

'Yeah, we believe him,' the girl said again. 'It's just that we've got nothing to say.'

'*Nothing*?' asked Tom incredulously.

'No. You're doing fine. Honestly.'

'Well,' I said, trying to drag something out of this. 'Will you commit to telling Tom when you *do* have something to say?'

They all said 'Yeah!'

One glanced at his watch, without bothering to disguise the fact.

I knew they were not telling the truth. All of us in that room did. But this team were not really talking to Tom. They were talking to The Boss, and all Bosses, deep down, were not to be trusted.

Tom was stuck. So was I.

I thought of all the sick companies I'd worked in over the years. What 'medicine' did they need? There was so much pain in the organizations I met, not usually as extreme as Tony's bitterness, but a sort of a dull, low, tooth-aching pain born of frustration and boredom and half measures. So much was being left unsaid, as Tom had found, by people who couldn't or wouldn't speak. Yet, clearly, only they had the power to act, to change. It was ridiculous for people to expect that the very bosses they hated would make things better, yet that seemed to be the hidden assumption. So many people in organizations seemed content to make the best of a bad job, too focused on what wasn't right to be happy, too content with their lot to change.

I remembered visiting my home town recently and being given a leaflet marking the 150th anniversary of the building of the Town Hall. I realized for the first time that our coat of arms bears the motto: industria omnia vincit – work conquers all. Considering it is a Northern mill town whose boom came in the 19th century, the original meanings seemed clear. 'If we all work hard, we will break the chains of poverty or idleness; the Protestant work ethic is good for God and society.' But my work in organizations, meeting so many passionless or hurt or confused people, made me feel there was another meaning to that motto. That, for many, work has conquered all: it has gained victory over choice, over will, over responsibility, over our dreams, over our life. Work has come first, life is second. We work to live. Far from setting us free, work has made addicts and prisoners of us. Addicted to the organization for our fix of money and for a sense of purpose and structure in our lives; and imprisoned by our own limiting beliefs about words like work and business.

There was no sense of energy for change in these organizations. For many, even Tony, it was bad, but nowhere near unbearable enough to consider an alternative. The habitual pain wasn't strong enough to be a motivator of change. Nor was the pleasure. I'd seen people form their own companies backed by little other than faith, passion and barely a thousand pounds in the bank. And then they had sat back as their success came and watched as the thousand pounds grew fat and multiplied into millions, whilst the faith and passion, untended, withered and died.

Nothing buzzed or hummed with life in the organizations I worked in except the faxes and the forced jollity of sales directors. Companies were inert systems, safe and predictable: they had lost all the fire in the belly.

Where does the fire go?

It was easy to see what was wrong with business. We only need to bring a part of ourselves to work in traditional organizations. Our hearts and spirit, our souls, are left to be nourished by that decreasing amount of time we call our own. But they are not – because we don't have the energy left. All our energy has been channeled into withstanding pressure and drudgery and maintaining a straight line which we call 'the bottom'.

Offering a solution to this problem was more difficult. Perhaps Heather was the solution, and we could all be rich on it. But I remembered Heather's words about true change coming inside out and that left me with a challenge: how do you get someone to accept that they are a prisoner or an addict? And that, once again, brought

me round to thinking about my own life. What were my chains?
What was my drug?

There was a phrase going round my head, something about
compromise and cowardice going hand in hand. I couldn't tell,
however, whether the phrase applied to my clients or to me.
Everything seemed connected. I couldn't think of a concept such as
'business' or 'the organization' without thinking about me – not
from an ego point of view, but from the simple understanding I was
now developing: that if I could not change myself, how could I
expect anyone or anything else around me to change?

'A Friendly Disclaimer' read the brochure.

'Although St James's Church, in its openness of heart and
mind, includes, Alternatives, the ideas in the Alternatives
Program are not representative of the church itself.'

From my pew near the back of the urban cathedral in central
London, I gazed at the ancient dark wood, stained glass and
vaulted ceiling. It was unmistakably a Christian place of
worship, although the program of workshops and lectures
presented by Alternatives ('dedicated to exploring new
consciousness') seemed a universe away from my own
upbringing as part of an aging, white middle class Church of
England parish in West Yorkshire. *Psychic Protection; Kahuna*
Wisdom; Hundredth Monkeying; Global Therapy – these things
were not available in All Saints, Churwell where I worshipped
as a child. But here in St James's, you could listen to *Ecstatic*
Poetry whilst God in his Trinity peered down from the
backdrop above the altar. And you could come to hear Heather
Campbell, Shamanic Medicine Woman, give a talk entitled
Death: As A Beginning as Christ crucified died in the wooden
sculpture on the wall.

So was Heather's stuff to do with religion? How did her
spirituality fit with mine? Though, to be fair, there wasn't
much of mine to fit with. A regular churchgoer until I left
home to go to university, I had lied to my father years later
when I took him on a tour of my college. He had asked about

services held in the chapel and I'd mumbled something in embarrassment – to be truthful I didn't even know what the chapel looked like inside. I took him to the bar instead. As a schoolboy I'd enjoyed the dressing up and paraphernalia of church-going. I remember being convinced that God sat behind the altar cloth, even though that would have put Him in the car park. I remember thinking that our vicar was somehow otherworldly and special, until, one Sunday after evensong, we gave him a lift home and, as he got out of the car, he caught his cassock tie in our bumper and we yanked him off his feet into the gutter. At times, I took the services very seriously, talking and praying into the black void behind my closed eyes; and some of the psalms were so beautiful they made me want to cry. But I really didn't feel that anything was happening to me. Other than this, religion had only made one brief return to my adult life when I wrote to a girlfriend who was trying to break up with me. I'd contrasted my desperate state with the evident faith of a priest I'd heard preaching at a funeral. But it didn't do any good. The girlfriend took my angst for self-pity – understandably, because it was – and left in any case. And I didn't have the girl, or God.

So, since this seemed to be the sum total of my spiritual life, I was confused as to why I still felt guilty sitting in an Anglican Church about to hear a Jewish Medicine Woman talk to us about death. Was I being asked to replace my failed religion with a new object of worship?

And let's put the lapsed-Christian bit to one side for a while. What was I doing here, a business consultant? What was I looking for? Because I was beginning to feel that this quest for a new consultant for our company was turning into a search for something for me, or in me.

My hunch was difficult to express and even scarier to think about translating back into the rational, secular world of organizations in which I earned my living. Undeniably, there was a new movement towards what was loosely turned 'spirituality in business' – the *Harvard Business Review* had even published an article exploring 'New Age Management'.

Boeing were employing a poet, Lotus had a 'soul committee'. *The Soul of a Business* had been a best seller and Anita Roddick claimed to be making profits with principles. But overall, the whole area of spirituality in business was difficult to get to grips with. I felt that the people who were doing this were as confused by it as the rest of us. The 'spirituality' was something about values, or purpose, or meaning, or was it ethics? Above all, it felt like a grafting on of one thing onto something else and the critics saw that. Tom Peters famously dismissed it as 'an invasion into our private lives' and others cynically pointed out it was probably just another way of getting people motivated at work. Spirituality in business was easy to dismiss as a passing fashion. Was the fact that Heather had walked into our lives just another manifestation of this 'trend'? And would it pass, as the skeptics predicted, when we consultants moved on to the next management fad in our search for an answer to all organizational ills?

Perhaps this talk would answer some of my confusion. But to be honest, I couldn't imagine what death had to do with business.

Heather was introduced and took up position center stage. She was smiling and made a joke about her clip-on microphone. Her mood didn't seem appropriate to the subject matter.

'Thank you all for coming. I really did not expect this many people. In fact I thought a talk on death was probably equal to commercial suicide, so I'm terribly happy to see you all here.'

I looked around. For the first time, I realized that there must have been a hundred or so people in the church.

'So, first of all, who am I? Well, I am a strange mixture. My religious background was Orthodox Jewish, my upbringing was middle class Scottish and my very first career was in the theater as a Stage Manager. I was one of those people that really wanted to be absolutely necessary for something important – and a Stage Manager is definitely that. But, I also wanted to be in a corner in the background and not seen by anybody. And SMs are that too. In fact, the only time they are noticed is when something goes wrong. But that was who I thought I was.

'It has taken me many, many years to realize that was a lie. I do want to contribute to something important, but I don't want to be hidden in a corner. It was shamanic self-development that brought me to that realization. And I suppose the reason that I'm telling you this is because that part of me died. The Heather Campbell that liked to be in the corner and never seen, died.

'That was a huge death for me. And I must say I really like the rebirth. I do like myself more now then I ever have before.'

We all laughed with the reborn Heather.

'As I was preparing this talk, I asked myself – how does one become qualified to talk on death? It takes guts to stand here and talk about death when you haven't physically experienced it yourself. So why am I qualified?

'Well, from the age of about three I used to collect bones and skeletons and skulls; I loved bones, they fascinated me. So I started with death early. But having a love of skulls and bones doesn't exactly give you a qualification. Probably the main reason that I find myself talking about death is because death, physical death, has come to me many times in this lifetime. It's almost a little embarrassing to admit, but, in fact, several lovers of mine have died.'

Heather chuckled. I squirmed. How could she talk about death in such a relaxed way? For me, this was a taboo subject – and if you'd lost a lover, that was something to be met with sympathy, even silence – certainly not laughter.

'In fact, I was about to be married to the last gentleman who died. He died five weeks before my wedding.

'But I had a choice about how to deal with this. There was part of me that definitely saw the funny side of it. I could have gone into self-pity – asking why God was punishing me with this.

But, what I came to see is that death is part of my destiny. This is something I'm good at: I'm good at people dying. It's a strange gift, perhaps. But for me, in this life, this time around, death is why I'm here. I get to experience it a lot and then pass on what I've learnt to others.'

I could sense from my fellow audience members that we were in agreement. Heather Campbell was qualified to speak on death!

'I went on to study anthropology and that's where I discovered shamanism. I found that a major part of shamanism was honoring death as equal to life and this is the basis of my discussion tonight. The dictionary says death is "cessation of life" – I don't agree with that. It's only an ending of *physical* life, a cessation of the cells and the blood and the body. Death is not an ending but a transformation. It's an in-between state that leads to rebirth. Most tribal peoples have this same belief system, honoring death as equal to life. Any people that live in harmony and balance with the natural world always see death as equal to life because when you live in nature you know there cannot be spring without winter. You get reminded of that year after year. Winter is a death, but death in the plant world does not mean that it is a cessation of life; it simply means that it is part of the cycle that is followed by rebirth.

'In Native beliefs, death is called a "give away" – whenever something dies it "gives way" to something else that is alive. Let me give you some examples: in nature, if an animals dies, what happens to it? It's eaten by other animals: it helps to give life to another. Or the old leaves fall from a tree, and as they decay, they turn into mulch, and provide the very necessary minerals and trace elements in the earth which help new trees to grow. Nothing ever ends. The whole of life is a movement, a coming and going, of energy. So the main thing I want you to realize about death is that it is part of a cycle, not the end of a straight line. The second thing to learn is how to feel differently about death.

'Why is there so much fear of death? Death-death – by which I mean the death of the physical body – is the only experience all living creatures will share and yet it is still shrouded in mystery and fear. You'd think by now the human race would have come to terms with this eventuality, but that doesn't seem to be the case. Our technologies have taken the chance or mystery out of previously inexplicable events. A computer can help us predict an outcome before we act. We can see the child in the womb before it is born and know its sex. But death is still a mystery. And that's why we are afraid.

'All fear is of the unknown. Stepping into the void without faith is scary. Death and change are similar because both make us afraid and both are resisted. In fact death is a change and change usually involves a death ...'

And with that word *change* I began to hear Heather as the business change consultant as well as the spiritual teacher.

'Death is natural and inevitable and necessary for something else to be born – and so is change. Death happens all the time and change is a constant. These things are true. We experience "little deaths" every day of our lives, whether at work or outside work. At the very least, our skin decays and our hair falls out every day. But there are other deaths in every aspect of our lives. Changing your mind is a death, losing your virginity is a death, leaving home is a death, getting divorced is a death, getting married is a death, having a baby is a death, changing your hairstyle is a death, starting smoking is a death – '

Heather paused whilst the audience laughed.

'– *stopping* smoking is a death, ending a relationship is a death, changing job is a death. Anything that means we are doing something that we have a fear of, something we have never done before, something that is new, that is a death. So why not get used to it?'

For a moment, I felt like Heather was speaking only to me.

'So you have a choice about all those constant, inevitable changes in your life. You have a choice about how you see them, how much you resist them, and therefore how easily you let the new thing be birthed.

'To be asleep in this world, to stay fearful and resistant to change is to stay in the box into which you were put by your personal history, whether that's the working class box, or the uneducated box, or the academic box, the religious box, the sheepish follower box, the egotistical leader, the bully box, the victim box. We get stuck in boxes like these through fear. Life offers us change. We may be offered the way out of something, for example, or given the chance to do something we have never done before – but fear stops us and we refuse to take the risk. We have to allow the part of us that resists to die – in the faith that what results will be an improvement.

'That little, quiet, mousy stage-manager-me that nobody noticed died. It was the part of me that was scared to take my power. That part of me was asleep. Maybe there are parts of you wanting to die that you don't really want anyway! Parts of you that inhibit you stepping into your own power, parts that you cling to just because you know them – and anything known, no matter how painful or dark, is going to be less scary than what is unknown. But let them go!

'I urge you to turn your fear into excitement – to jump into whatever abyss confronts you. Because if you jump into it with joy and excitement there *will* be a rebirth – something will come out of it that is more powerful, more exciting, happier, more centered than the part of you that you allowed to die. And it is like peeling back the layers of an onion – the more you peel away, the more you let the safe old you die, the more true to yourself you become.'

It was late Monday evening in a church in central London. All over the country, people were going to sleep – another little death – exhausted and stressed and confused about the changes taking place in their workplaces and their lives. Afraid of what change might bring, scared they might not be up to it. I thought of our firm, a group of consultants, like many others, trying to eliminate the fear, trying to 'manage change' by measuring and modeling and anticipating. I thought of our change management methodology, trumpeted in our brochures and proposals and hustled in front of a thousand client companies, a grand model of inputs and processes that almost made us look like we were worth the fee. And I realized that our methodology had nothing of 'joy and excitement' – as Heather implied change could and should have. That's because no-one in business – least of all us – seemed to be joyful or excited about change. We had proved to ourselves that we were living in the most interesting of times, but, like the Chinese proverb, we saw ourselves as cursed in doing so. If everything was getting so much better – faster, more colorful, more varied, more technologically effective – and if there was so much more knowledge and information at our disposal, than why was the prevailing mood I sensed in business that of anxiety and not exhilaration?

And me? It was easy to point the finger at everyone else. But where was I going to get my 'joy and excitement' from? I realized that my happiness was founded on a deep wariness of change. I liked things to stay the same, providing I was still moving up some sort of imagined ladder towards more money, more power, more and better quality things. I divided experiences in my life into good and bad. Bad experiences were anything that delayed my momentum up the ladder. The purpose of life was to avoid bad things happening.

To live a life that considered all change as joyful and exciting seemed madness and an evasion of reality. Could I ever sell such a vision to a client? It was scary to consider it. It would be a risk to try. It would be a change. A death. Did I have the courage to jump into the abyss?

Heather was finishing her talk.

'I'd just quickly like to return to that thing about fear of death. I know that people are afraid because they're scared of the unknown. But I also believe that fear on the deathbed is based on regret at not having manifested the dreams of one's youth.'

I was a youngish man educated at Oxford, from a loving family home; I had a good career ahead of me, a big car, a beautiful wife and a good sense of humor which meant that I was good at making people like me. And most of the time, certainly more often than not, I thought of myself as happy. So what would I have to regret?

The sound system suddenly crackled and popped. Lights dimmed and then flashed for a moment.

'Oh, oh,' said Heather. 'I'm being buzzed from above ...!'

I smiled.

Later that night, I called Heather to thank her for the talk.

'You enjoyed it? Good,'

'Hugely!' I admitted. 'And what a great finale – real rock star stuff!'

'Oh you mean the flashing lights? Yes, well, don't worry about it; weird things happen when you talk on death. It was probably my dead friends wanting to get in on the action.'

I waited for a while.

'You're not joking are you?' I said.

'No. It's good to listen when you hear voices, Bill. It might be dead friends, or it might be a better part of you – your Higher Self. Who knows? Either way, they might have something valuable to say. And anyway Bill, those lights might have been flashing for you, not for me.'

I laughed. I didn't know what she meant.

'I'll call you soon, Heather. We must take all this to the next stage.'

'That would be nice,' said Heather.

But it was not to be that simple.

THE WEST: PLACE *of* PHYSICAL BODY CHANGE *and* TRANSITION

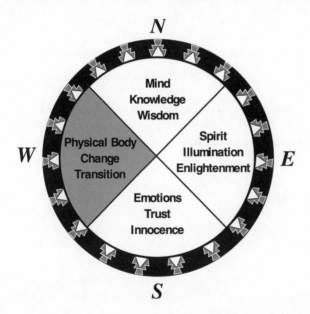

Shamanic healing is a journey. It involves stepping out of our habitual roles, our conventional scripts and improvising a dancing path. The dancing path leads us from the inertia of sleepwalking to the ecstasy of living the spirit of the moment. Too often our lives automatically get channeled into narrow, secure patterns, set into deadly routines.
Some of us want out.
Some of us want to let go and wake up to the power within us.

Gabrielle Roth, Maps to Ecstasy

I said my hellos to all and sundry as I walked down the corridor towards my office. My PA was on the phone but gestured 'Hi!' as I passed. There was something the matter though. I had a good sense when things were about to go wrong, and the look in her eyes told me something was up.

Maybe she'd seen what I now saw on my desk – a brown envelope marked *Internal Mail*. You didn't see many of those nowadays.

Not unless ...

I sat in the office of the Human Resources Director, but she wasn't there. Summoned to hear the terms and conditions of my redundancy, she wouldn't even show me the decency of attending my interview.

Instead, the task had been delegated to an assistant, some junior personnel officer. I was furious, my anger keeping at bay a rising tide of panic about what was going to happen to my life.

The girl had a clipboard on her lap. I could see that the top sheet of paper was headed 'Termination Guidelines'. As she rehearsed to me the various factors involved – 'complete restructure' – 'your department not the only one involved in the redesign project' – 'decision has been made at the highest level' – I realized that I could read what the guidelines said. I was good, I found, at reading upside down writing. Some of it read:

KEEP THE MEETING BRIEF

DON'T BE DEFENSIVE OR ARGUMENTATIVE.
DON'T BE APOLOGETIC.

REMAIN CALM AND TRY NOT TO DISPLAY ANY
EMOTION

HAVE KLEENEX AVAILABLE

USE SILENCE TO ...

I realized she was waiting for me to say something.

'I'm sorry,' I said. 'Could you repeat that last bit?'

'I was outlining the one alternative. You can take the full package now or you can be seconded to us as a contractor on a two day a week deal.'

'Two days?' I said. 'What do I do with the rest of my time?'

'It really is the only option. Or, as I say, you can take the clean break.'

Even I was surprised at how quickly I decided. Before she could say any more, I took the non-clean break, and agreed to work on a per-contract basis. This would take up a fraction of my former hours and yield me a fraction of my former salary. But I was grateful to snap up anything that offered a measure of continuity and security.

I don't think I have ever been so scared as at that stage of my life. For days, I vacillated between fear and self-pity, but most of all I felt anger at my treatment. It was not fair. I deserved better than this. My wife Grace offered love and encouragement, but my depression made me dismiss it as patronizing advice. How could she know how bad I felt?

The redesign of the company had taken me completely by surprise. I knew something may have been in the offing, but not this soon. Paul had been offered a new post in Japan, developing groupware technology as a learning tool. His future sounded a lot more defined than mine.

The company knew they'd have been wasting their time to give me an overseas posting – I'd made it clear I'd done enough traveling when I was younger. And now with a wife and plans to start a family, I wanted to settle in this country. So to an extent, I suppose, I'd brought this on myself by my own sense of priorities. Was there anything else I should or shouldn't have done? What could I have done differently?

I spent many lunchtimes over the next few weeks meeting old friends and contacts. The old network seemed healthy. The prevailing opinion amongst the people I spoke to was that I would have no difficulty in finding another good job. All this should have comforted me. The shock of redundancy, however, had left me wounded and with growing feelings of self-doubt.

Paul's leaving had disturbed me the most. We'd worked so long together that I felt we'd built up a close working relationship. But the voice of doubt in my head suggested that it was not truly a partnership of equals.

I should have realized it earlier: Paul had been the strongest partner. I just played second fiddle.

I know a career consultant who counsels people, usually men, usually recently redundant men. Instead of moving straight to the CV, to shuffle and update achievements and responsibilities, she goes back to something deeper. She takes her clients back to their dreams, back to the hopes and visions they had for themselves before their career stacked up like luggage around their lives. She also looks at their values and beliefs. And then she checks how relevant the vast majority of their working life has been to those values, and those visions. The sadness, she says, in most cases, is that this is the first time they have been able to express their dreams, or to look inward at who they really are. And the double sadness is that they're usually in their late forties before they are given that opportunity.

I thought of calling her up, because I could have done with making that sort of review of my life. But something in me felt embarrassed at the prospect of calling her; it would have been an admission of failure.

Then, one night, I knew that I should speak to Heather. Perhaps I was looking for rebirth rather than counseling. Heather had spoken about leaping with joy into the abyss. Whilst the redundancy certainly made me feel that an abyss had opened up in my life, I was a long way from looking forward to the leap.

When I visited Heather and told her about the redundancy, she didn't offer commiserations as people usually did. She just asked me how I felt about it.

'Sick,' I admitted. I was slumped in one of Heather's armchairs, feeling very sorry for myself. I watched a coat of milky froth dissipate on the surface of my coffee.

Heather nodded, more in acknowledgement of my feelings than in agreement with my point of view.

'Think of how many people have been thrown into a similar position over the last fifteen years,' she said. 'That amount of downsizing – that's what you call it isn't it?' She paused and glanced over at me with a turn of the head to check she was correct.

'"Downsizing" is one of the terms for it,' I responded, glumly, without looking up.

'That amount of downsizing has got to be happening for a reason.'

'It's happening,' I snapped, 'because of cost cutting and technology and ...'

'No, I mean from the point of view of the people concerned,' Heather said, ignoring my temper. 'Some of the greatest healers have found their gift only after dealing with personal disability or affliction. The adversity was the condition that allowed them to discover what they could do, although they too began by cursing their bad luck. Many people have learnt, ironically, to be grateful to their organization in making them redundant. How many personal dreams have been born on the back of a big payoff?'

'I don't feel like thanking my company.' I said, shaking my head.

'Because you haven't found your new dream yet. You will. At the moment, though, your option must be to learn what you can from your experience.'

I remembered one of the Star Maiden's questions: *What are the teachings I am here to learn?*

'The change in your company is a death – the death of the old structure, of that era of the company. It's a death for both Paul and for you in terms of the end of your partnership and old career paths,' Heather said. 'It's a sign that something better is going to be reborn. Something new will replace all of those dying things. You've just got to trust that. Face your fear and deal with it. It's a primary tenet in my path that you need to face what you most fear.'

'I feel like I've cheated a bit then, taking the two day a week option. You'd have told me to have taken the plunge, I'd bet.'

'Maybe,' she said. 'Just be conscious of the choice you're making. If you're taking the safe option just because you're scared, then I don't think it will turn out for the best in the future. But there are things you can do with the remaining three days: you'd said that you wanted a chance to observe more of my work. Well, you asked for it – you got it!'

We laughed, her more than me.

I said 'I've just become aware that Paul took many of the real decisions in our partnership. He overpowered me a lot – or I gave in to him too easily.'

'You see – you are learning from your experience,' Heather said, with encouragement in her voice. 'This is time to address the parts of you that need work – to take your own power!'

'Hmm. The more I think about it, you know, the more I did give in. I'd always hold back on saying what I really thought ...'

'Well you would do that!' interrupted Heather, excitedly.

'Why?' I asked, surprised at her animation.

'Because you're a Do-Gooder, Bill.'

'I'm not sure whether that's supposed to be a compliment or an insult.'

'Neither – it's a character type we were taught in the Deer Tribe. It suggests that everything you do comes from wanting recognition, acceptance and approval from others. You look to others for something you should be finding in yourself. The most important thing for a Do-Gooder is to be liked, therefore all your reactions will come from that place. As a result, you'll always be a nice person to do business with.'

I put my coffee down and I sat back, waving my hand in front of me to dismiss what she'd said. 'You're making me sound like that character I once saw in an American sketch show; he used to say: "I just wanna be loved, is that so wrong?"'

'Yes, well, that's a good question,' said Heather, thinking about it.'Is it so wrong to want to be loved? Actually, it's not about being right or wrong in a moral sense. If you're on a path of self-development, you must ensure that everything you do, every interaction you have with others, is being done for the right reason. And the right reason is not to be liked by them, because being liked is not always the best thing for everyone. For example, a good friend is someone who will tell you something that is very hard to hear, and that might put your being liked in jeopardy, temporarily at least. The good friend will say it anyway, because the truth is better for everybody, in the longer term. But a Do-Gooder wouldn't take that risk; they'd keep everybody smiling and think it better not to rock the boat.'

'But Heather,' I replied, mock hurt, 'my mother always brought me up to be nice to people, to be polite.'

'Yes, most people were,' she agreed quickly, 'which is why there are a lot of Do-Gooders in the world. We were not brought up to honor our individuality of self. So your happiness depends on what other people think of you.'

'But that's a reality,' I said, convinced I was right. I sat forward to give weight to my comments. 'You get on, particularly in business, by controlling the impression you have on people. That's why there are so many influencing skills training programs around!'

'And that's flawed for two reasons,' she replied, utterly unfazed by my argument. 'Firstly, you can never ultimately control other peoples' perceptions and interpretations. And secondly, it means you're always giving your power away to other people. You're never really yourself, you're just what you think you ought to be.'

'But it gets results,' I said with emphasis.

'That's what the trainers will say,' Heather said, following my tone of voice. 'But does it? Think of the most powerful people you know – and I mean by powerful the strongest, most independent people. You know they don't really care about creating the best impression. They care about doing the right thing for the situation at hand.'

'Yes, but ...'

'Most people, as I say, are not brought up to honor their individuality of self. They are given certain parameters that they are supposed to act within. That includes social niceties and moral niceties. Walking a path of self-development means looking again at all the things we are encoded with. Yes, if you're young and healthy, for example, it is appropriate to give up your seat on the bus to the old age pensioner – but is it appropriate to tell white lies in order not to upset somebody? Your mother makes you a meal of liver and bacon for twenty years even though you hate it, but you never say anything. Is that better than telling her the truth and preventing her wasting all that time and energy on cooking a meal you loathe?'

I was sure I would never do anything that stupid, but didn't think about it too hard, just in case.

'It's that thing I keep coming back to,' Heather explained carefully. 'Short-term pain, long-term pleasure; long-term pain, short-term pleasure. We stay with the lie because we think we're choosing pleasure, because it's painful to tell the truth. It's potentially embarrassing, hurtful to the other party and therefore damaging to our reputation. So we lie. And we justify our lie – "it's only a little thing, it's only a meal of liver and bacon." But the end result is always a worse one, because every time you go there to eat, you're going to have to lie again, you're going to have to eat that awful dinner and your mother is going to have wasted her time again. Your mother could probably cook fifty other meals that would please her *and* you.'

It seemed to me that Heather's ideal of the Impeccable Warrior would be a grumpy character, never pleasing anybody else.

'Many people on my path have been called selfish,' she said in agreement with my thoughts. 'And the Warrior Path is indeed a self-focused one, because you are totally involved with yourself – your actions and reactions, your thoughts and feelings. You're constantly being aware of everything you do, asking yourself why you've done it and examining the outcome so that you can do it better next time.

'But this isn't so foreign to your world of business. You have process reviews at the end of meetings, you have appraisal sessions to look back on what you've achieved and how you've achieved it. But you only review actions, rather than motivations, or thoughts and feelings. The problem is you don't do it consistently and regularly enough, you don't make reflection a habit, so you lose the Warrior's capacity for anticipating results based on self-awareness. Process reviews and the like are organizational substitutions for what we all should be doing for ourselves.'

I thought about this. Maybe appraisals and process reviews don't happen as often as they should – even though everybody agrees they're a great idea – because people get embarrassed talking about themselves and how they behave. It's always easier to talk about impersonal things like objectives and agenda points.

'So I should be more selfish and less nice?' I still wasn't convinced, because all this felt like a reversal of everything I'd been brought up to believe. As a result, I wanted to reduce everything to black and white. Heather didn't rise to the bait.

'My path is based on self-responsibility,' she said with firmness, 'because the only thing you can take responsibility for is yourself. The only thing you can easily change is yourself. You can't take responsibility for, or change, someone else's feelings or actions or beliefs any more than you can take responsibility for the weather or for your cat. So, yes, in that sense, the Warrior Path is a selfish one. That's why Warriors are difficult people to have around: since most people are conditioned to telling untruths, they're not used to hearing the truth either. Warriors make them uncomfortable and then defensive.'

I took a drink from my coffee. It was cold, but I didn't say anything.

'So I'm a Do-Gooder then? What are you?'

'I'm a Fart.'

I perked up. 'Hey, I thought a Do-Gooder was bad – a Fart doesn't sound too good at all!'

'Farts kill to be leaders, and tend to have large egos. Nobody can criticize a Fart worse than they can criticize themselves, so we do a really good job of undermining ourselves and we're our own hardest taskmasters. Nobody's as hard on us as ourselves. But we really don't care what other people think, we do and act as we think appropriate and to hell with it if people have a problem with that. You're the nice people to be with, but we tend to be the leaders.'

'I know a few Farts,' I said.

'Remember these are just labels: it's not name-calling. This is about self-responsibility, Bill. People have to learn to take responsibility for how they respond to things, they have to take responsibility for what they think and what they feel. If I'm hurt because you tell me I'm a Fart, that's my problem, not yours. I've got to learn what that hurt might be telling me ...'

I sighed. 'But, Heather, there's still a part of me that's thinking, how bad can it be to want to make other people like me.'

'Well, that's your decision and it's not a dreadful decision. It's a choice you make about how you want to develop, and whether you want to become clearer on who you really are and what you really want. When you start on a self-development path, you're a long way from finding out who you are, but, with thought and reflection, you might see that a lot of your habits and conditions are not actually you, but have been imposed by others on you. So you gain an inkling about who you *aren't*.

'You may make a decision that says "this is how I am" and not wish to change, and that's fine. But it's very hard to be in the world of consultancy and not want to change and improve yourself – because you can't teach to others what you don't do yourself. And unless you're an Enlightened Being, you've still got some things to learn. The more you learn in your personal life, the more you'll be able to help other people learn. That's why consultants can be the worst of influences, because they have the nerve to go out there and tell companies how to improve and change, but they won't look at the negativity and bad habits and patterns in their own lives. They are fakes. How can they share with someone what they haven't gone through themselves?'

After leaving Heather's house, I drove into the High Street to draw some money from the cash machine. I parked up and left my car straddling the pavement and road near to some traffic lights. I waited in the queue outside the bank and gazed back down the road, thinking about Do-Gooders and Farts and Consultants. My attention was caught by a small, battered red car inching through a gap between a lorry and the side of the road where my car was parked. It was obviously having difficulty moving through that narrow space and I was amazed that there could be people around who were so impatient as to put themselves under that much pressure for so little gain. But it was now my turn at the cash machine and I turned to key in my PIN number. In that moment, for those brief seconds, I forgot the red car – and then remembered it in the very next moment when I heard a soft KTHUD. I knew immediately what had happened. As if in compensation, five crisp, new £10 notes slid out from the machine.

I sighed quietly, took the money and turned to inspect the damage. What did I feel? Angry at the driver's stupidity. Hurt at the damage to my beloved new car. Frustrated by the delay and inconvenience that this idiot was going to cause me now and in the next few days whilst my car was being repaired. Out loud, very deliberately, I said: '*Shit!*' There was no way I was going to be a Do-Gooder about this. I was furious and I was going to let whoever was responsible know it.

The driver got out of the car. He was a young man, wearing a suit. I thought of him immediately as an estate agent, for some reason. He looked very worried. As he began to speak, I held up a hand to stop him. In my head I was screaming at him.

'It's OK,' I said. 'Don't worry.'

The man smiled. 'Thank you,' he said. 'Thank you so much. I thought you were going to shout at me.'

So I was a Do-Gooder after all.

———————

As I drove away, I found myself laughing.

I remembered what Heather had told me once about Spirit sending lessons for you to learn and some were heavy and some were not too heavy and that the great thing was you really began to appreciate how cunning Spirit was in that respect. If the event outside the bank had been set up by Spirit, I could see what she meant.

Spirit's up there – wherever there is – and he – or she – or it – is thinking, 'OK so Campbell's told him about Do-Gooders and he sort of accepts it in his head, but he doesn't really believe it in his heart. So why don't we let him experience what she was on about?'

So Spirit sets up a car crash, just a small one, nothing too dramatic – 'and we'll make it in Surbiton just so he knows that he can learn anywhere, any time, he doesn't have to be in the desert or on a mountain top or on peyote.' Fair enough, a small car crash. Bound to get me worked up and emotional. Bound to make me feel like taking it out on someone. And what happens? I melt. I give way. I yield. "Don't worry," I say. Nothing to worry about!

I also realized I'd been given another teaching as a bonus. If you choose to park in a shitty parking space – next to a traffic light for example – make sure you're prepared to take responsibility for your actions.

Nice one, Spirit.

My thoughts moved on to what Heather had said about self-development. Because in the end it didn't really matter whether I agreed with her about Farts and the like. It didn't matter whether the two categories she'd described to me were totally comprehensive or just useful generalizations. What mattered was what she implied: that if we can identify our chosen pattern of response to certain situations, we can open up to the possibility of choice and self-change ...

I realized that this was a chance to improve my life, not by gaining more but by getting rid, not through the accumulation of things, but by the giving away of the habits and patterns that brought me pain.

Everything I'd done up until now had been a journey into the material and secular world, where I'd picked up honors and qualifications and attachments and symbols of power to show how well I was doing. And from the perspective of society, I was doing well – or rather, I was doing what was expected of me. An education, an income, a house, a marriage. That was what it was all about and I was fulfilling my obligation to society. From that point of view, I thought, my life had been a bit like jail.

I drove through the tree lined streets of commuter-belt towards home, passing the usual milestones of the journey along the way: a petrol station, a supermarket, a sofa warehouse, a golf range. I slowed down in the two areas where cameras checked my speed. When I looked down at the road ahead of me, littered with rubbish and litter and burst tyres, it seemed to disappear with astonishing speed beneath my wheels. I was moving very fast down the road, and there seemed to be a lot of junk in the way.

Over the next months, it was not clear whether I was making any progress in clearing up the junk.

The incident with the car had affected me powerfully. In conversations with Heather – and myself – after that episode, I'd made a commitment to improve my life, not in terms of enhancing a work-related skill or competence that would bring me more money, not in terms of investing more time into a hobby to have more fun, but to improve in a general, holistic sense. I wanted to discover what it was I truly wanted and to uncover all the habits, beliefs and attitudes that were stopping me getting it. I wanted to take responsibility for my life.

This was in itself a huge change for me. I'd been conditioned to think that any talk about 'the meaning of life' was either abstract, philosophical, intellectual masturbation or stoned hippy shit. Even worse were the purple robes and glowing auras of the New Age movement. All three of these stereotypes for me were 'way out' – way out of any sense of practicality or use. There was a fourth also – the viewpoint of religion. Whilst I was moved by the Church's music and prose, I was left untouched by its message. So I had four places from which to consider life and its purpose and all of them left me uncomfortable. There was in me much resistance to seeking a deeper, broader understanding of the mysteries of life.

I came to accept that my family upbringing had a lot to do with this reluctance, although in a surprising way. My family, I thought, was profoundly normal. We were Church of England, and the values I was taught by example were Christian, chiefly consideration and service to others. Behind these were a commitment to politeness, good manners, cleanliness and smartness in appearance. Don't be selfish. Share. Don't boast of your achievements. I remember, when I was going to university, a friend joking that I should do an MA in being nice. Above all, my background was practical and grounded in everyday life. There was little tolerance for extremes or deviance. Perhaps it was natural that I had little patience for introspection or ideas of enlightenment.

I had never questioned if those same values, so common and decent, could be the source of some of my present dissatisfaction; that service to others, for example, could overbalance into the disempowerment of Do-Gooding, that humility could be itself a form of ego. Or that my adherence to the everyday had left me with no contact with the extraordinary and magical in my life.

I began to realize that I had created my life and everything in it through the filter of who I was; and yet who I was had largely been shaped unconsciously many years before. If I now wanted other things in my life, I would have to change the way I thought, felt and acted. I would have to change my conditioning.

This was to be a personal quest, but I still thought about it like a consultant. Working with Heather had helped me to understand that it was fruitless to talk of 'organizations' as if they were anything other than collections of individuals; as a result, I saw organizational problems reflected in my personal experience and vice-versa. This was no exception. As I had done in my own life, organizations had designed out diversity in favor of conformity and homogeneity. Focusing everything so closely on a single arbiter of success – the bottom line – they had left no space for magic or spirit. Organizations were like my upbringing had been – safe, comforting, with all sense of danger removed. Without the danger, Heather had implied, it was impossible to get the magic. But it was also impossible to graft magic onto a company – or indeed fun, energy, creativity or good service. Those things had to be released from the inside, from people.

I launched myself onto my own quest for magic in a habitual way: I treated it with all the gusto and drive I'd been taught to apply to any decent consultancy project. One of the first wise things I learnt was that the journey was more important than the destination. That was a good thing, because I was enjoying spending time in book shops. I was vaguely embarrassed at first in standing in front of shelves marked *Self Help*, as if I thought asking for help was some sign of weakness, but as time went on, my familiarity with these books, and their assurances that they were 'No 1 best-sellers', made me sure that they would give me what I was looking for.

And this seemed definitely to be the time to be doing this. The sheer range and choice of books that claimed they would change my life was astonishing. I noticed that some of them were crossing over into other areas, so that in one book shop I might find a self-help book in the business section, in another the psychology section, in still another I'd find them in a huge display in the window.

Clearly, other people were searching for something too.

So I bought books and I read.

I found myself drawn in particular to those books that promised big results in a very short time. I liked phrases like 'control/master/run your life' 'quantum change' and 'unleash'. And I loved timeframes such as 'now!'. In the self-help literature, I noticed, the word 'now' was always followed by an exclamation mark. I was drawn to 'tools' and 'technologies' and anything that suggested it was a science, because these concepts implied that there was an almost mechanical solution out there.

But overall, I was disappointed and confused. My purchases would leave me excited and enthralled, but not changed, not for long. I'd have moments of clarity and insight but then I'd fall back into old habits and conditionings. Resolving not to get angry when things didn't go my way, I'd make huge efforts to think positively, breathe deep and remain cheery. Mantra-like I'd do my silent affirmations: *I am a calm person, I am a calm person. I am happy.*

The search for failsafe techniques was proving a hard one. And more than anything, I felt that I was even farther away than before in understanding three of the key terms in the whole human potential movement. I was unclear as to what *Achievement* might be, or *Success*. And *Happiness* was a bugger too.

I left the cab and pushed through the revolving doors into the lobby of the central London hotel. On the noticeboard to the right of the reception desk, red plastic letters spelled out both the name of the seminar I was holding and the room it was to be held in. The name 'Montpellier Suite' suggested something grander than the dingy, ill-lit basement room I was escorted to, but I was used to the constraints of the budgets of those who employed my company. I was also familiar with the attempts of conference hotels to squeeze every inch of revenue out of their available space. This particular room was less a suite than an annex to the kitchens. It certainly smelled of cabbage.

I drew open the blinds and looked out onto the fire escape, the refuse bins and, towering behind both, the severe brick wall of an adjacent office block.

I was here to run a workshop on change management for an established client as part of the per-project contract under which I was now employed. Their company, like most, was facing extraordinary pressures for change both from within – in the form of reengineering projects – and from the marketplace – in the form of increased customer power. The focus for this session was on establishing the behaviors that this particular senior team would have to exhibit in order to convince the rest of their company to follow them willingly into an uncertain future.

Easy. There was an established methodology for doing this.

I began setting up, taking a pile of acetates out of my briefcase and drawing up boxes and charts on the flip chart. A young Italian waiter in a grubby white shirt and false bow tie came into the room carrying two pots of coffee and, next time round, a plate of biscuits.

He asked me in poor English if there was anything else I needed. I looked around the room at the brown walls and blue, sixties, stackable chairs and told him no.

My group arrived in dribs and drabs over the next fifteen minutes which made some of them two minutes early but the majority of them about ten minutes late. I made small talk with some and waited patiently until the last attendee had arrived and had emptied the second coffee pot.

Eventually, we were ready to start.

I began as I always did with suggesting some rules for the day, ('which rules can we break?' I joked) both operational rules – times of lunch and breaks, smoking – and process rules – how we wanted to behave and treat each other during the workshop. As usual, the first two words suggested by the group were 'open' and 'honest' and I wrote them up on the flip chart unquestioningly.

After about an hour I noticed the effects of the coffee wearing off and attention in the group wandering, so I threw in an icebreaker exercise to cheer everyone up. As the morning wore on, I passed round forms to fill in, gave them games to stimulate ideas and split them up into working sub-groups to brainstorm solutions.

We wrote words down and we crossed words out. And, above all, we argued over the meanings of words. The meaning of 'empowered' gave some of the group particular difficulty. I noticed how it triggered them into thinking of boundaries and limits, rather than freedom and choice.

'Well, we don't want chaos, you know!'

I suppose they were being open and honest with me.

Just before lunch, the chairman took his jacket off and hung it over the back of his chair. Immediately, five others did the same. After a few moments, I did too.

A small voice inside me said: 'biggest change so far today.' 'Shhh!' I thought to myself. 'Concentrate!'

By the end of the workshop, the walls of our little room were covered in flip chart paper, bearing the messages and ideas of eight corporate minds. I began the ritual of filtering the mass of material down into action points and then, when we'd haggled and debated what they were, assigned initials to each one. This denoted ownership and was supposed to ensure that the recipient carried out that particular task.

But I knew already that nothing fundamental was changing. Some of these action points would get carried out, undoubtedly, and some of them were excellent, valuable ideas. But many of the changes proposed here would get lost amidst the constant noise and pressure of real day-to-day busy-ness. Other suggestions would fall by the wayside, untended and ignored. They'd end up on meeting agendas for months to come, gradually slipping down the page until, one day, unnoticed and unmourned, they would slip into the void of good ideas that never went anywhere.

And as for behavioral changes, I knew that it was always easier to envision how you'd like to be than shift the habits ingrained into your behavior over years of practice. These people were clever. They'd got to the top of their company through behaving in a particular style, and, realistically, were unlikely to give that up now. It had, after all, got them exactly what they wanted. And they were the last ones to understand the pain that continuing in that way was going to cause their company and everyone connected with it. It was easy for them now to write a statement of heartening values, as we had done that afternoon, and send it to all their colleagues with a promise that this was the way it was going to be from now on. But I was looking into their eyes now, and I knew that I had not shifted anything much inside them. Maybe I was being too harsh. Maybe some of them genuinely believed that their public commitment to change and a written document with their signatures on, was what it took to make things better. But that was even worse for me, because I had done nothing to disabuse them of that belief. I'd told them all the right things, taken them through all the case studies, models and tools on which my company's strong reputation was based. I'd even told them to 'walk their talk' which I thought would amuse Heather, because I knew the phrase had Native American origins. But telling them was one thing. Hearing it was another. Doing was still another. We were asking them to learn to walk differently – in a way that reflected their new talk. That was a profound personal change and I knew I hadn't delivered it. I didn't know how to do it. We had talked a lot about change, but I had not taken them into it.

Amidst the debris of the day, amidst the flip chart paper and blutac and empty cups and full saucers and stained table cloths, the chairman offered me his feedback. 'That was excellent, Bill,' he said. 'Really excellent!'

'I'm delighted,' I confessed. 'Are you staying for a drink to talk through the next steps?'

'Erm, well, I'd love to, really, but I've probably got a lot of messages waiting for me back at the office.'

He patted me on the arm.

'Next time, yes? But well done. Really excellent!'

He walked off. I began to collect my acetates together.

I looked out again through the basement window at the brick wall and the fire escape that seemed to lead nowhere. I wondered how I could ever have hoped to get these people genuinely to see into the future, into the unknown, when we were closed in by such a dead environment.

As for me, on that afternoon, I felt as if someone had switched a light on. It was no excuse that the client was apparently satisfied with the workshop. I didn't know whether I was pleased or disappointed or ashamed by the feedback. I did know that it was relatively easy for a consultant to impress a business person. All it needed was sound argument, plenty of strokes for encouragement, the correct vocabulary for credibility, an enormous safety net of case studies and reference sites and a couple of games to make them understand that we were as inventive as our brochure said we were. Everybody had done their bit, everybody had played their roles, everybody was happy. Except me. I was selling the client short, selling the world short, selling me short. This was another, unexpected result of my conditioning. I was a Do-Gooder. I wanted to make people happy, even if I knew that what I was doing to make them happy in the short term was doing them no good in the long. This client – and thousands like him – needed something dramatic and profound if they were to achieve the level of change they were looking for. If it was dramatic and profound it was going to be scary: but I was too afraid to push them – or me – into it.

I felt confused and doubtful, convinced that what I'd done until now was insufficient, yet blind to how I might supply something worth while in the future. One thing was clear, however. My heart was no longer in my work.

In the taxi on the way back to my office, where I would report the success of the day and make plans for tying the client in to the next huge program of consultancy, I read a couple of pages from one of my new books. There was a quotation from Boris Pasternak:

The great majority of us are required to live a life of constant, systematic duplicity. Your health is bound to be affected if, day after day, you say the opposite of what you feel, if you grovel before what you dislike and rejoice at what brings you nothing but misfortune. Our nervous system isn't just a fiction; it's a part of our physical body, and our soul exists in time and space and is inside us, like the teeth in our mouth. It can't be forever violated with impunity.

Up until now it had been easy for me to say that I could put up with any amount of 'systematic duplicity' at work. I could be as political as the next person if it got me my way. I could schmooze or kowtow when necessary, I could be economical with the truth. Apparently none of this behavior, so alien to what I thought of as my 'true character', cost me anything. And I could easily suppress my feelings and intuition, because those parts of me were not to do with work. They were for my not-work life. I could play the often silly and sometimes vicious rules of the business world, because that was the way things were, that was how you got on. And since it paid for all your ambitions outside work, it would be foolish to complain about it. It was easy to be duplicitous if the salary kept coming in.

But today had shown me a different dimension of duplicity: performing work that did not relate to my conscience, that did not align with my principles. And I was being praised and rewarded for it into the bargain, so that it would have been perfectly acceptable to carry on. (Nice one, Spirit!)

The last twenty years had seen an upsurge in ideas from management writers about how to make organizations into healthier, looser, more stimulating, rewarding and fair places. But now, I saw, there was a deeper problem, which goes beyond organizational design and theories of motivation. It is the way we have been conditioned to separate life and work. Putting work into a box, the place you go rather than what you do as part of your life's purpose, the transaction in which you earn the money to do 'what you really want to do' – that separation is at odds with the desire to live a life characterized by ideas such as balance and harmony.

It was only today that I began to wonder what sort of effort it took to keep *work* and *life* separate in this way, and what the results of that effort might be.

One beautifully sunny summer evening I drove to the railway station to meet my wife Grace on her journey home from work. I parked in a space, but with only 10 minutes to go to 6.30pm took the risk of not feeding the meter. Instead, I kept the keys in the ignition, put on a favorite tape, and unrolled the soft top to my sleek red sports car. And then I waited, leaning – no, posing – against the bonnet, taking in the sounds and sights and smells of commuting London. Men in shirt sleeves and loosened ties, women in colorful, fine clothing, the whole scene suffused with the glow of lightness that the occasional sun encourages us to feel. It's the end of the working day. It's summer. Life is good.

I remember seeing Grace in the distance, amidst a crowd of people, stepping off the escalator. My heart seemed to leap, which I took to be a romantic sign, a big, soft thud in my upper chest. And then my heart began to race, which was more unusual. And it didn't stop racing. All of a sudden, the scene in front of me was just the same, except that someone had turned the sound down. I was suddenly very aware that I was inside my body looking out. It was eerily quiet. And my heart continued to race, now pulsing, now fluttering. It made me feel very sick.

Then Grace was right in front of me but somehow still nowhere near as close as the me inside my body, the me crammed in beside my pounding heart and a burgeoning sensation of fear.

'Bill,' I could see her say. 'What's the matter ...?'

'I used to see one patient every couple of months who had some sort of stress-related condition,' said my doctor, writing something down on his note pad. 'Now it's, well, two or three each week.'

He looked up suddenly.

'You're just one of that number. You're working too hard, or working too long, or both. You're worrying about your job, or your boss, or your mortgage.'

He jabbed at me with his pen.

'Or you're just worrying. The worry's eating you up ...' slipping into his American idiom.

I wondered what a New York doctor was doing practicing in South London.

'... and you need to do something about it. You need to stop doing whatever it is you're doing to yourself. But what do you want me to say? Take a month off work?'

For a moment, I thought he was actually going to give me such permission.

'But I can't do that! If you don't work, you'll lose your job!'

He laughed.

'I'll have you booked in for an ECG, make sure there's nothing physically wrong with you. But there probably won't be. There's no history in the family, is there?'

I shook my head.

'No, I didn't think so. It's stress. It's not your heart that's the problem.'

I was not ill. But I was not in health.

I'd have felt happier if I'd have been able to walk away from the doctor's surgery and say 'Yes, he's right, I'm worrying about such and such.' But I couldn't. The obvious candidate was my situation with the job, but I knew that wasn't what was wrong with me. I was still, despite Heather's counsel, terrified of being left without work, without a job to go to. I still felt betrayed and angry. But that was not the source of my discomfort, that was not what had caused my heart to flutter and race in stress.

My intuition was speaking to me now. It was a low, quiet voice from deep inside, so far inside and so long unheard that it was difficult to catch everything that was being said. But my intuition made me feel that one single event, however prominent, was not responsible for my dis-ease. I realized that there was a whole series of things out of joint in my life.

It was easy to list some of them. My life had been built around doing well, whether that meant at school or at work. But everything, suddenly, had gone wrong. The job that had provided an underpinning of security, the basis of our hopes as a future family, was now, literally, in fragments. The principle on which so much of my career had been built – that change in organizations could, eventually, somehow, happen outside in – was flawed. And the very elements of my character which I thought had contributed to my popularity and success had also now been shown to contain the seeds of my current downfall.

I took the afternoon off work to reflect on what was happening. The thoughts raced in my head – all of them offering different dimensions to the problem as much as offering any solutions. And I tried to deal with things in distinct parts. To combat any possible heart problems, I was already making resolutions to cut down on the beer and join the gym. Again. For work problems, I decided to approach a headhunter and get a job, quick. I didn't take my reflections much further, however; soon after arriving home I fell asleep on the sofa.

I dreamt I was back at school although I didn't recognize the surroundings. There didn't appear to be a school building. Instead there was a huge field, dotted with desks, some of which had Bunsen burners on them. So this was a science lesson. And there was Mr Newell, my physics teacher! He was on a unicycle, steering it precariously down a plank of wood. Every so often, he would fall off into the pools of mud at either side, but that didn't stop him leaping back on and trying again. It seemed important to him to get the lesson across. In the background, for some reason, Mr Stanley the Geography teacher stood tutting and shaking his head, drawing on his pipe. 'You daft bugger!' he said to me.

I came to in a daze and sluggishly pulled myself off the sofa. Hours had passed since I'd returned home from the doctor's. There was a note on the coffee table beside me. It was from Grace, telling me she too was home now and down in the kitchen.

Grace had put a pot of soup on to simmer. It smelt glorious, waking me up together with my hunger. I walked downstairs to join her.

In the kitchen I saw only her feet at first, pointing straight up at the ceiling. This was her yoga practice. Recently pregnant, Grace had decided to start now on preparing her body for the huge changes it was about to undergo.

'Hi!' she said, looking up at me from the floor. 'Come on down! It's good for the heart, you know!'

'You shouldn't joke about these things!' I snapped.

'Oh, Bill, cheer up! Look –,' she dropped her legs, rolled onto her bum and then stood straight up in one long, flowing movement, '– do a simple exercise with me. I'll bet it'll make you feel better ...'

'No thanks'

'Come on. Just one. It's great for stress!' She laughed again.

I decided to humor her.

'All right. Just one! As long as it doesn't take too long and as long as it doesn't hurt.'

'That's the spirit, yogi man!,' she laughed. 'OK. Try this one – it's easy. All it is is sitting down.'

I followed her as she placed herself into a simple cross-legged position. 'All you have to do is sit straight and balanced. You're trying to sit on your coccyx, in fact. It'll help if you pull your bum cheeks apart.'

I did so, shuffling from side to side. Then Grace talked me through the next stage.

'Good. And now drop forward and slowly come back up. Try and get your spine as straight as possible, by placing one vertebra upon the next, step by step, until finally your head falls naturally into place.'

I seemed to have achieved that.

'Bill. Look at your shoulders – feel how tight they are.'

As my attention moved to them, I realized my shoulders were scrunched up with tension. I let them drop and, as I did so, the whole of my chest area opened up.

'That's good!' said Grace. 'How does it feel.'

It felt glorious. I felt completely grounded, my whole weight falling through the center of my body to rest on the floor. But at the same time, I did not feel sluggish or inert. The way my chest opened up seemed to fill me with energy. I realized that a lot of the time, it had become natural for me to hold most of my tension in my neck and shoulders, thus keeping my torso shrunken and closed. Each part of my physical body, sitting there on my kitchen floor, felt at ease and in its right place. I was in balance.

I enjoyed the sensation for some long minutes. I suppose I wasn't changing the world here, but it was a great experience for me personally. I had two thoughts. Firstly, at how profound the change had been when I focused on my body, rather than worrying about my thoughts. Secondly, I realized how powerful my thinking had been. My mind had almost prevented these moments of peace happening, by projecting images of embarrassment or stupidity. I'd always thought of the mind as at the top of the hierarchy when it came to the various human aspects – after all, without the mind, you couldn't do much. But these last few minutes showed me that thought had its limitations, shortcomings which were as potentially painful to the health of the whole person as a strained muscle was in the physical dimension or a broken heart was in the emotional one. Thinking could get you into trouble and keep you from recuperation. There seemed little point in continuing to value the mind above all the other aspects. Maybe they were all as valuable as each other.

I sat there wondering at how I'd resisted even trying yoga, amazed at how my own laziness and torpor had almost kept me feeling from this sense of energized calm. I wondered how I might be resisting a natural urge towards balance in aspects of me other than the physical. What was I resisting mentally, emotionally or spiritually in my life?

As I meditated on all this, I realized that my original terror at the railway station, when my heart had begun that fearful race, was that I was facing Death, the Grim Reaper. But I was not. Perhaps it was more realistic to assume, in Heather's terms, that I had experienced the death of an old part of me.

My attention began to shift on to what would be born out of it.

———

Recuperating further that night with a beer in hand, I watched an old *Colombo* movie on TV. Peter Falk shuffled his way through the episode, parked his battered old car in all the wrong places, stubbed out his unlit cigar butt in all the wrong places, and always made sure he was in absolutely the wrong place at the wrong time for his prey, the murderer, staring him down with his one good eye.

Those anti-hero habits and trappings are one of the reasons I've always liked Colombo, far more that any other of the American detective series, the Mystery Movies. Kojak – too smart by half. McMillan and Wife – too Seventies Playboy. McCloud – what's the point? Colombo's different. Colombo's a pain in the back side, an annoyance, but a wise fool, the knowing idiot. He wears his antagonists down with relentless naiveté – 'oh, sir, just one more thing' 'there's one thing that's been bothering me' 'sir, I just don't understand' which is in contrast to the smooth artifice of the dissembling criminal. But it's a trick, just the same. I used to think that I would have liked to have been him.

And then, that night, beer in hand, I realized why I already was like Colombo.

Because the one unchanging thing about Colombo movies was that he always came into the movie a third of the way in and spent the rest of the time trying to find out what the rest of us already knew. He comes in late and tries to catch up. That felt like me, now. I felt like I'd come into my life late, and was trying to put it all together again to make sense of the mystery.

Grace and I were invited to join some friends of ours for dinner at a riverside pub in Oxfordshire. It was a balmy summer evening with a fresh cool breeze.

I'd been expecting to be there in an advisory role. Philip, a co-worker of mine had mentioned some time back that his wife Becky – something in finance at a European bank – wanted to grill me about how you got into change management, since she was getting frustrated in her job 'and wanted to work with people not numbers.' She was not alone. In fact, in just that last month, three people from my network of contacts had coincidentally contacted me, all of whom had expressed a desire to move their careers into training and development. In the last two years I'd probably only spoken to one person who'd shown that sort of interest. Now three in a month. The other interesting fact was that they were all female. That felt like a pattern, not a coincidence.

For Becky, I couldn't see any immediate connection between accounting and training and development, but I was certainly willing to help. Unhelpfully, I'd rehearsed a little joke about perhaps training accountants to be more interesting, but in fact I didn't get the chance.

'Oh no, Bill,' said Becky. 'Things have changed a bit since Philip spoke to you. I've been offered a redundancy package – and I'm going to take it!' She reached across and grabbed her husband's hand, as if she was going to make an announcement.

'We're going on a round the world trip!' she said, smiling. Philip nodded too.

The whole group of us cheered and offered our congratulations. I had only a long holiday in mind, so I must have looked shocked when they told us they were going for eight months.

'Eight months?' I said. 'Wow! That's amazing! But what are you doing about your job, Philip?'

'It's worked out really well, actually,' he explained. 'I told my bosses what the situation was and I asked for a sabbatical.'

'A *sabbatical*?' I said, even more astonished. 'I thought only academics did that nowadays. Didn't they mind?'

'No, well they didn't show it if they did. I went to see the Human Resources Director, and she said: "You may never get another chance to see the whole world like that. Take it now!"'

'That's just wonderful!' I said. 'Congratulations again.'

A part of the old me would have been bitter at the seemingly unfair treatment of Philip and me by the same company. I would have brought the image of that human resources person to mind, and kept it there until I began to seethe and sulk, eventually ruining the evening for everyone else as well as me. But I felt curiously open about this news. It felt like I'd been meant to see that experience is what you make of it, rather than what you let happen to you.

We spent the rest of the evening probing Philip and Becky for details of their trip – what route they'd take, how they'd travel, where they'd stay. We reveled in feeling envious – but it was a light, playful envy shot through with sheer joy at the experience they were going to have.

So many deaths around. So many rebirths.

The next morning, before leaving for a meeting with Heather, I shared a coffee with Grace and Emma. Emma was a friend of ours who'd discovered she was pregnant just two months after us. I sipped my coffee whilst they demolished a packet of biscuits.

'It's bizarre,' said Grace. 'I was on bananas last week. These cravings are so strange. It's like you really, really want something. So you go and get it. Then, as soon as you get it, you think "That's not what I want!"'

I know that feeling, I thought. It describes how I've been feeling about my career.

I looked at Grace and beyond her, at a noticeboard we have on our kitchen wall. Pinned to this were cuttings from various catalogs and magazines of things that over the years we were convinced we'd want to buy at some time – hooded bathrobes, stain-resistant floor coverings, a special brush for getting cat hairs from the carpet. I walked over and perused the cuttings, some of which were yellowing and curled with age.

One said: *Magnetic Massage Insoles will change your life!*

Really? I thought.

One size fits all. Trim to size. Also effective against foot odor.

'I've realized: Paul was the one I acted most Do-Gooderish with. Now he's gone, I don't have to do all that pleasing. I can concentrate a bit more on who I really am.'

I was telling Heather about my experience with yoga and the various insights I'd had over the last few days, particularly about my relationship with Paul.

'When you were talking about Do-Gooders, I thought the only other option you were implying was to be rude or self-centered. But now I realize that I was wrong. I thought I was a martyr to Paul and everyone else. I thought my role was to serve others and make sure everyone was OK and ensure that the ship was steady. That was just a cover for me not doing the best I could. I always had a good excuse not to be as good as everyone else, because all my energy was taken up in pleasing others.'

'You were giving your power away,' said Heather, smiling in agreement. 'Think of it this way. On one level, we are, like all things, a vibrating mass of energy. Self-development is about trying to increase our vibratory rate. To do that we try to eliminate those things that drain our energy and cause its rate to decrease.'

She took a sheet of paper from a drawer and began to draw simple lines in pencil.

'Here you are,' she said, turning the paper round so that it was facing me. 'Let's say God or Great Spirit or The Universal Creator gave us each ten units of energy. Many people use, oh, four units of that available energy maintaining a bad relationship, one based on attachment, comparison and characterized by poor communication.'

She crossed through four of the lines.

'They use another two units keeping in their anger and resentment about their boss and co-workers.'

She drew diagonal lines through two more of the marks on the paper.

'Another two units are used in hating their job. Not only do they hate the organization and the people that make it up, they actually hate the work too! But they say they have to do it for the money, so they carry on hating! So eight of their ten units are being used on maintaining pain.'

She drew a large black circle around the eight crossed out lines and underlined the remaining too.

'That leaves only two units to find happiness. Those are not good odds! And it's not the wife's fault, or the boss's or the job's fault that they're so unhappy. It's their own fault because they're the ones who are giving away their power to all that dark stuff in their lives.'

She started shading in the big circle.

'It's a heck of a change for me to redesign my energy into something more productive and beneficial,' I confessed, looking at her diagram and mentally redistributing the ratios. 'It's scary.'

Heather looked up from her drawing.

'Yes, it's been a death and a rebirth – in fact, many deaths and many rebirths,' she agreed, listing them on her fingers. 'A change for Paul – a leap into the abyss of a new job. A change for you – a leap into the abyss of being independent. And a change for me – the death of my relationship with Paul and Bill and the birth of a new relationship with you.'

I saw that all of that was true – those were the new births from that single death.

'I was terrified about this redundancy before,' I said, 'but from the perspective that it has happened to help me, rather than harm me, it feels like I could succeed.'

'Only if you actually change the way you think and behave,' Heather said seriously. She got up and wandered over to the large patio doors that opened out into her garden. 'I think most people, deep down, know exactly what it is that's causing their stress or unhappiness. It's a questioning of accepting that realization at first, and then finding the power to do something about it.'

She stopped to greet a pair of jays that had landed in her birdbath.

'But for you,' she continued, not looking back at me, 'the great thing is you've picked up your first arrow.'

'Huh?'

She turned around. 'Remember the night I taught the Star Maiden's Circle?'

'Yes.' I conjured up the wheel of symbols and signs in my mind's eye, but Heather was already 'drawing' it in the thin air in front of her.

'The South East is the place of self-concepts. If I ask you how you see yourself, whatever you respond is a self-concept. Many self-concepts derive from our personal history and in particular from your childhood and what you heard and saw about yourself then. And we are updating our self-concepts all the time. When something happens, we choose our response, and that choice becomes our action and colors our perception of what continues to happen.

'Now, a major part of self-development is changing our self-concepts so that we can see ourselves as who we really are – not as we have become accustomed to seeing ourselves because of how others have treated us in the past. Other peoples' perceptions of you are rarely "the truth", since they are colored by their own personal histories or their current mood.

'You should ask yourself: "What are my self-concepts: do I feel good about myself or bad?" because the answer will explain a lot about how you use your energy and what life you create for yourself.'

At first I understood what Heather meant not in terms of my personal life but in terms of work. I thought of a client of mine and a particular department I'd worked with. That department – although they played a crucial role in the success of the company – saw themselves as the scapegoat of the company, saw themselves as put upon, unappreciated. They were bitter with everyone else. In other words, as a department, they had appalling self-concepts. And they were performing less and less well. It was easy to see how limited an individual would be with similarly derogatory self-concepts.

Heather continued:

'The place of the South East is divided up into various arrows, which symbolize how we choose to express our energies in the process of life. There are seven arrows of the light, colored by pleasure and responsibility, and seven arrows of the dark, colored by pain and reaction.'

I was intrigued. 'Is this metaphor of arrows part of the Warrior concept,' I asked keenly, 'arming yourself for battle and so on?'

'Yes, but it's present in a lot of cultures,' she said, closing the patio door and moving back into the room. 'The Bible talks about "put on the whole armor of God", the "shield of faith" and so on. It's a magical garb and in neither case are we talking about human wars, because the Warrior path has nothing to do with violence or destruction. But it is about struggle – the struggle to be free from personal weaknesses and limitations.'

Heather was down on her knees now searching through a bookshelf. She brought out a book showing a beautiful Native drawing of seven arrows held in a decorated quiver. She pointed at one of the arrows and said:

'We say that self-awareness is the first weapon you'll need to do battle against some of your shortcomings. It's being able to stand apart from yourself and examine your thinking, your motives, your actions; that's how you become aware of what needs to change.'

Heather's finger pointed across the full range of the quiver and stopped on the seventh.

'You're aiming to pick up a full six arrows so that you automatically gain the seventh: Impeccability. Then you'll have the warrior's freedom, you take your own power rather than giving it to others, you are in alignment with all forms of all things, and you are at cause in your life. You are never at the effect of anyone, anywhere, at any time, in any way.'

Heather paused for a moment. I think she must have seen how serious and reverential I was looking. She picked up her pencil again and bopped me on the forehead with it.

'And you make full use of the warrior's discipline of humor, which means you never take yourself or life too seriously.'

I rubbed my head and smiled.

Heather began to flick through the book for another drawing, which, when she found it, I saw to be equally beautiful but darker.

'Unfortunately, most of us are going to be more familiar with the Seven Dark Arrows that create Ego Self-Importance,' she said. 'These are the arrows you must identify in yourself and eliminate, because they'll always disempower you, no matter how natural or normal they seem to be to your character, or how common in other people. Ego Self-Importance is where we're caught in a self-destructive pattern of continually having our buttons pushed by everything that happens – be it the weather, the boss, the situation or other people's behavior. Everything else is at fault; the whole army is out of step except us.'

I shrugged my shoulders and gave Heather a look which said 'Yup, I recognize that!'

'Is all this familiar, then Bill?' Heather asked, smiling. She closed the book and returned it to its place on the shelves. 'Ego Self-Importance means that the majority of our energy is spent in defending our self, in caring for our self-image – whether that's trying to demonstrate that we are the best or most worthless, that we are the most beautiful or the most miserable, the most successful or the most unlucky. Taking a path of self-development means that you stop focusing on the ego and what hurts or benefits it. And you start focusing on the appropriate use of your personal energy, your personal power. You shift from victim to creator, from being at effect of things to being at cause. The focus shifts from outside in to inside out.'

I remembered that Heather had used those terms back at the IOD when we were talking about change in companies, but I was more interested in applying these insights to my own life.

'Life is a choice,' Heather continued. 'If you're starting on a path of self-development, you pick up the first light arrow of self-awareness. Only through self-observation is one even aware of *having* the seven dark arrows – let alone working on them.

'It's almost like turning a light on, it's like a light switch. When you're asleep in this world, it's as if you have a pencil beam torch showing you the way ahead – you have to follow that narrow beam of light because it's all there is. When you turn on that light of self-awareness, you suddenly realize that you have a whole 360 degrees of directions that you can choose to walk in. You see yourself within a larger framework. When you become aware of how you fit into the greater picture, your perception of everything that happens to you in life changes. You begin to see with the eyes of an eagle – surveying everything around you. With the pencil beam, you see only with the eyes of the mouse, only ever seeing what's right in front of your little nose.

'When you have that first arrow you'll start seeing things differently – just as you have tonight. The deaths of your company being reorganized and Paul leaving are wonderful for you. It's a gift that Spirit's given to you and you are just beginning to see this very positive perspective on the experience. But if you hadn't begun to pick up that first arrow, if you'd have been following that little pencil beam in a straight line, then those same deaths would have been terrifying for you – they would have taken away all the security of that sure, safe, steady thin beam.'

'They were terrifying! And it still is a bit!' I admitted, honestly.

'What you most fear you most need to face. Shamans work by pushing you into the abyss – to overcome your fear through facing it. Fear is a limiting factor.'

My attention jumped at her words. I remembered that was a phrase I used to say myself.

'Fear is a limiting factor!' I intoned, grandly. 'I used to say that when I first came into business. I used to do presentation skills training. The people who came on those courses were always so nervous, so afraid.'

'And what did you tell them about their nerves?' asked Heather.

'That it was a natural thing and a good sign,' I replied. 'It showed that they were getting excited and that their adrenaline was pumping. I told them that they could learn to use that adrenaline to help them perform better.'

'But what did you make them do to help them to deal with their fear?'

I stood up to show her and strode around the room.

'I got them to breathe differently,' I said. 'And I used to make them move – change the way they stood and walked around.'

'That's right,' she said, watching me parade up and down. 'You overcome your fear by going into action, as opposed to being paralyzed by the thought of what you're scared of. Your level of fear increases in direct proportion to the amount of energy you give to it.'

I nodded excitedly.

'Yes!' I exclaimed. 'When it was their turn to present they'd just sit there. Nobody ever wanted to go first – they seemed to prefer sitting and thinking about how awful it was going to be.'

'I know what you mean,' Heather agreed. 'When I used to go through lots of ceremonial initiations, my fellow students always thought I was brave because I usually volunteered to go first.'

She pressed down on the table as if to make the point clear. 'It was understanding the benefit of facing fear, not courage, that always made me the first to jump. I realized that standing in line and *thinking* about what scared me was much harder than just "going for it".'

'Do you think that's true of working on yourself?' I wondered.

'Yes,' nodded Heather. 'Self-development and fear are bedfellows, but as you begin to accept your change and growth, your perception of fear as something to be avoided will shift. You will start to see it as a valuable teacher that provides you with an opportunity to grow rather than with a justification for giving up.'

I'd always considered myself something of a coward, consciously choosing to avoid things that scared me. Funnily enough, as a boy I had a fascination for horror films and ghost stories. Perhaps I focused all my fear into the world of fiction and tried to avoid it in reality.

Heather took the sheet of paper on which she had drawn, folded it neatly and put it back into her drawer. She glanced across at me.

'Don't give up,' she smiled. 'By working on yourself, by waking up, by becoming a lighter person, every interaction you have with those around you will be lighter. That's the best validation of all because changing yourself will affect your wife, your dog, your business colleagues and the man in the car next to you. As you become a happier, more controlled person, less at effect and more at cause, everyone about you will benefit from that.'

Over the next months, my self-awareness became like a muscle which I developed with exercise. I became an observer of myself. I found I became better at identifying the way I got myself into positions where I had to say what I didn't feel, or take on someone else's responsibility out of a need to earn their respect; thus I built up a clear picture of when I was allowing myself to be a Do-Gooder.

At first, my self-awareness developed with hindsight. After the event, I would realize how I gave my power away. But with time, I found I was getting closer and closer to the moment in which the Do-Gooder in me kicked in. Eventually, I found I was at the point where I could step in and act to make a different choice, *before* I repeated the pattern, by asking: *who am I really doing this for, and why?* Hindsight was turning into foresight. I felt like I was creating a life, rather than reacting in someone else's.

My increasing confidence generated other exciting changes in my life.

I found I had the time, and, more significantly, the self-belief, that I should reawaken an old dream and explore the possibility of writing as part of my changing career. The old me would have dismissed such a thought out of hand, not because I was better at making judgments then, but because, I realized, I was better at closing things off. The old me was better at rejecting new ideas if they sounded in any way impractical. Logical analysis would have proved that there was no time for writing, so it would have stayed as how it began, a childish fantasy.

It was not easy to write, at first. For weeks I struggled even to find a suitable subject to explore. In time, I learned to write about anything and everything, whatever my imagination seemed stimulated by – holidays, cars, beer, a diary. After these initial explorations, my ideas began to converge on a single subject matter and my attempts became more focused on the one project.

I had no idea where this new path would take me – it didn't seem to matter if I could get my work published or not. What did seem important was to feel ideas being created inside and then becoming manifest on the page. It told me that I *could* do something that I had always wanted to do, that the same energies of innovation, attention and discipline I had saved for the workplace I could also implement in my personal life. I did not need reward or recognition, at this stage. I was doing this for myself.

In turn, this increased my feelings of self-worth, and brought a new dimension to my self-concepts. I could now see myself as being creative, something I would never have described myself as. Creativity was something that I had put in a box, labeled *Only To Be Used for Generating Ideas In Brainstorms*. I'd confined it to a purely mental activity. I realized that creativity was not an act, but an attitude, a way of life. Creativity was about bringing any new thing into being – new ideas, yes, but also discovering new approaches, attitudes and feelings and expressing them in your behavior. Artists express their discoveries on the canvas, in the clay, or on the page. Others find their artistic output in their lives.

Grace and I had created a baby. I also felt I was creating a new life. Just as we had found that there were lots of fun and varied ways to make a baby, so, I accepted, there could be lots of different ways to live a life.

THE NORTH: PLACE *of* MIND KNOWLEDGE *and* WISDOM

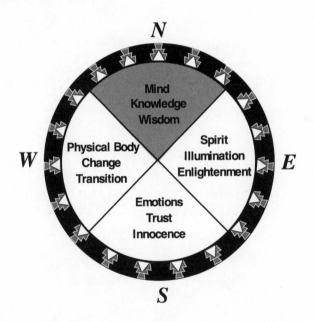

Pure logical thinking cannot yield us any knowledge of the empirical world; all knowledge of reality starts from experience and ends in it. Propositions arrived at by purely logical means are completely empty of reality.

Albert Einstein

My search in the book shops of London for a way forward with my life was still a frustrating one. I was becoming disillusioned at the promises, the absolute solutions, thrown out so carelessly from the covers of the self-help literature. That was because they were not being converted, at least by me, into a changed experience. And the exercises in these books, *Five Steps to this, Ten Stages to that,* seemed on the page so easy to do that I felt guilty when I couldn't make them work. I spent one too many evenings having to interrupt my visualizations because I couldn't remember what the next instruction was. Maybe I had to buy a book on memory. Or concentration.

Similarly, my developing self-knowledge didn't always uncover positive things such as my desire to write. I found that I didn't know how to relax. In my earlier years I'd done some theater and was used to the warm ups and guided meditations that we would take each other through before a performance. I was too busy for these exercises now, and I'd realized that I'd substituted deep relaxation for the quick fix of excess alcohol after a stressful day. Drink was not my only compulsion, however. I was addicted to worry. I worried about things I had done and hadn't yet done. I made hells in my head of things that might happen. I had little sense of judgment in terms of what things were truly within my power to influence and what things were the responsibility of others. For safety's sake, therefore, I worried about everything for everybody. I was definitely on the Worrier Path.

All the energy I gave to worry left me nervous, tired, irritable. This in turn led me to ridiculous bouts of temper, most often with those I loved. The only other option seemed to be to withdraw into what Grace kindly termed a blue funk but Grace and I both knew that the moods were darker and more bitter than such a description implied.

And all this turmoil was churning inside me under a calm exterior of confidence, politeness, and good humor. It was also in the context of relatively good social and material success. These many and deep states of dis-ease, peppered with feelings of great satisfaction when I got my own way (holiday, a certain film, the pub), seemed to be the sum total of my interior life. And no book seemed to be addressing my internal conflict. But over several months, Heather's calm insights spoke to me more and more clearly.

'Thousands of people go to psychotherapists,' said Heather, 'but how many of them would rather choose to buy all the text books on therapy so that they could learn what it actually was and how to do it themselves? Very, very few of them would, because we know that it's the relationship, the dialog, between the therapist and the patient that leads to insight and understanding.

'In a way that's the role I play with you. With me around you'll find it more and more difficult to kid yourself, or to be at effect rather than at cause, to blame someone else for something you create.'

'And I feel like we're dealing with what's wrong,' I added. 'Whereas the books are mostly about aiming for something that's right – some vision of success, some confidence or other.'

'The way to the light is into the darkness. It's what the New Age just hasn't got the hang of at all. Sending out glowing spheres of light and wrapping yourself in a rainbow aura! It thinks that if you don't give the dark any energy, then it will go away. That's just asleep, childish bullshit!

'The thing that uses your energy is the darkness,' said Heather with emphasis. 'Our energy is almost entirely used up by our angers, jealousies and greeds, even though they seem to make us feel better. But that's choosing short-term pleasure over long-term pain. Slamming the phone down on somebody, for example, makes the ego feel good for a time, but cutting short the interaction usually results in you spending all night dwelling on how angry or hurt or misunderstood you are. This pain drains your energy. No amount of solely concentrating on the light is going to increase your energy.'

Late that night, I came home and flicked on the light switch. A brief spark flashed into the hall way and somewhere up above a slight *PING* signaled that a bulb had blown. I pushed open the study door and reached inside to the light switch there, thinking that I could throw enough light out into the hall to be able to change the bulb. But nothing happened. Damn, I thought. Blown fuse.

Treading carefully so as not to wake Grace, I shuffled down the stairs into the cellar and groped around for the torch. It was not in its usual place. Maybe Grace had moved it. No, I thought immediately, *I* had moved it. In fact it was out in the garden shed now. Damn!

So I turned and peered into the inky blackness of the cellar. I tried to visualize the fuse box on the far wall, but nothing would come. Then as my eyes naturally adjusted to the darkness, the gloom seemed to lift. Within a few minutes, I felt confident enough to leave the doorway and step out across the dark cellar. Seconds later, I'd tripped the fuse back on and the room filled with light.

'You can't ignore the dark,' I said, explaining my little incident over the phone to Heather. 'But if you look at it long enough, you can begin to find a way through it.'

'Exactly so,' she responded, her encouragement almost palpable down the metallic phone line. 'It's great. You're now beginning to take the teachings into your home life, you're seeing them at work in even the most banal experiences. That's an extremely important stage. Workshop junkies never get that far. They never realize how to take all these teachings out of their notebooks and into their lives to bring improvement. They seem to be waiting for some sort of enlightened state or altered consciousness to hit them in the third eye and transport them to Nirvana. To my mind, this life, in this body, on this earth, is where we can make a difference. Sacred sites and spiritual workshops are not necessary for learning. With awareness, any mundane experience can provide us with self-knowledge. Taking care of your cat, doing your homework, or, yes, even changing a fuse.

'Be here, now. It's like the old Zen saying: after enlightenment, the laundry.'

I came home that night to find Grace in her workshop. She hadn't heard me enter the house, and I stood for several moments watching her work.

She sat on a stool in an arc of soft yellow light thrown out by the telescopic lamp attached to her workbench. Around her was scattered all the debris of paper and wood and glue and paint and scalpels that was the by-product of her craft.

I looked at her carefully as she focused intently on some minute detail I could not see. Motionless as she was, she seemed to be vibrating with energy, so completely was she engaged in the creativity of the moment. It was extraordinarily moving to witness. I knew beyond doubt that this was Grace's sacred dream, so clearly did she enjoy it, so obviously was she good at it, so evidently did it nurture and develop her. And moreover, her decision to create her own jewelry and crafts was being validated by the world; people were buying them!

I thought how much Grace herself had changed and grown since we had met Heather. I looked back over the years and her many attempts to find a job she liked. She moved from one organization to the next, from one industry to the next. It became clear that the world of organizations was not Grace's own best environment, but this growing realization showed itself as anger and self-doubt. So profound was her – and my – conditioning that 'proper' work could only be found in a 'normal' job, that we were both blind to the lesson that Grace should get out and find something new. On the contrary, she would not give up. She pushed ever harder to make each job work and I had made the situation worse by judging her a failure every time she had to leave. Everybody else could get their head down and get a real job, I reasoned. Lots of other people hated their work but tolerated it. Why couldn't she?

We would argue bitterly, hurting each other, not realizing that the most harm we were doing to ourselves was being dogmatic about the definition of the word 'work'.

When, eventually, Grace took her own power and began to develop her own business, even then my initial reaction was that arts and crafts could not be 'real work'. Since her enterprise was so small at first, this left her time to express her natural artistic nature in creating a home out of our house. I was astonished by her eye for detail and beauty and her ability to create something new from limited resources. I was proud of my wife, honored to live in a home that had such care and attention invested in it. Yet for months I struggled to accept that her capacity for designing and decorating was 'work' too.

For me, 'Work' had been the thing you did to earn cash; this cash you used to make your life enjoyable. Work and life were distinct elements. The end was the money and the work simply the means to the end.

Now, as I stood watching Grace, I realized once and for all that work could be an expression of who you are, that finding your sacred dream would generate fulfillment more deep and lasting than any financial reward. The big breakthrough for me was accepting that this was not a choice between sacred dream on the one hand and money on the other. If you were doing something you loved, something that you could genuinely put your heart and soul into, then the money would be there. This was an issue of trust.

'I don't have any financial worries,' Grace had once said to me, teasing my penny-pinching Yorkshire roots, 'because I don't worry about money.'

What lessons are you here to learn? the Star Maiden's Circle had asked. Here, I knew, were two: I was here to learn about *work* and *money*, because I had dark interpretations of both of them.

I realized that my becoming a management consultant, and now, more and more, an independent, self-employed consultant, was the ideal way for me to learn about both those subjects. I thought about it for a moment and felt a warm intuition inside me that all this really was true. I had not willed either the consultancy (it was a job I'd fallen into by accident), and I'd certainly not encouraged the redundancy (or, at least, I wasn't conscious that I had). Yet both had happened, and both had taught me lessons I would consciously not have chosen to learn.

I realized that there appeared to be a design to my life, a sequence of occurrences and events that, apparently distinct and independent, could be seen as a pattern with meaning and completeness. Even meeting Grace might be seen as part of this 'grand plan' – a way for me to extend my understanding of what work could be which I would perhaps not have achieved marrying a woman employed in a 'normal' job.

Was I in control of this design, this pattern, this plan? Or was it all entirely random?

At about this time, I became aware of a growing number of coincidences in my life. Friends and acquaintances who I thought had no connection to each other suddenly crossed each others' paths, and mine. Some of these synchronicities seemed transitory and meaningless. I bumped into an old college friend on a bus, miles from where I might have expected to see him. Others had a sense of fortuitousness to them. Discussing a promotional video for a colleague's advertising company in a pub one lunchtime, an ex- boss of Grace's walked past our table. He runs a video production company.

Still other coincidences appeared charged with significance, as if I was being given a sign that a particular decision or choice I'd made was correct. I'd grown in confidence with my writing and had thought about trying to have some things published. Meeting one publisher for the first time, we realized he had been on a training program I'd conducted years before. Then I found out that this publishing company was funded by an entrepreneur who I'd worked for in my very first job. These coincidences were startling enough. Then, one day, I booked a table at a restaurant in Soho to take a client of mine for lunch. It was near to Christmas and most restaurants were already full. The restaurant itself was my fourth choice and by the time they'd agreed to take us, the only table they had left was downstairs in a dingy far corner of the basement. So when that same entrepreneur, my ex-boss, walked in and sat at the table right next to us, I was not so much surprised as awe struck. My client thought I'd seen a ghost.

'Life's exciting!' I tried my best to think. 'It's not spooky! This is a good thing!' This incident left me realizing that I had no real idea what or who would crop up next in my life, and that was fine. As a chronic worrier, this was a big breakthrough for me.

'Acknowledging synchronicity is one of the first signs of waking up,' said Heather. We were walking through a park near my house. The wind brought a slight breeze that played like waves over the grass. We stopped for a moment to watch a squirrel run across the lawns in front of us and scoot up a tree; then we walked on.

'It's a way of accepting that you can learn from everything that happens, especially when events come together in the way they did with your publisher. It shows that your awareness has reached a point where it notices the things that happen to you and makes sense of them. But synchronicity's not about randomness and luck,' continued Heather. 'When people say they've experienced synchronicity, they are recognizing one of the Sacred Laws that all forms of all things are interconnected. Somehow your thoughts about video production, to use your example, go out as a vibration into the Everything and come back as the coincidence of you bumping into the film producer. Sounds woolly, doesn't it? I don't know how it happens but I know it does happen.

'Ancient cultures talk about this as manifesting reality through the power of words or thought. Their rituals and ceremonies were performed not to beg some divine power to make something happen. Their words and symbolic actions created a relationship, an alliance, with what they saw as a living universe. They expend energy to make the thing they want more likely to happen.'

'I read one of those "psychology of success" speakers once,' I told her. 'He was describing how to make a parking space appear for you near the supermarket entrance just be saying out loud that it would be there!'

'Exactly the same thing: manifesting reality through use of your personal power,' she nodded. We walked on. 'Isn't it strange, though, how people think of synchronicity as something that just happens to you "out of the blue" as opposed to something you create in your life.'

We stopped at a cafe to buy an ice cream. Some kids were playing nearby. About twenty of them formed a huge circle, linked only by their hands, and then, on someone's signal that

I neither saw nor heard, they all leaned backwards. Of course, connected as they were, they all supported themselves, even though the circle inclined so steeply backwards now that they were all gazing up at the sky. They all screamed with laughter.

Heather was smiling too. 'There is no separation between you and everything that happens out there.' She gestured with a hand movement that meant the universe. 'We are each a part of the web of life. How we perceive things affects that web. How we use our energy, how we live our life, is not exercised in a vacuum, separate from others. Our choices affect others. Think of the implications: it means that your life can never be boring and serious, because you are intimately connected to a living and ever-changing system!'

'I'll be honest, though Heather,' I said. 'I haven't yet fully understood that concept. I know that Newtonian physics was about separation – looking at distinct particles and their component parts. And I know that the new physics is proving that the universe is better thought of as flows of energy and the relationship between things rather than the things themselves. But am I really at one with the universe, a part of everything? I know the atoms that make me up are part of a universal system, but what about my thoughts, my actions. They say a butterfly flapping its wings in China can cause a volcano to erupt in Brazil. Do I really have the same power? It's still a difficult one to accept.'

Heather could see I was thinking it through. Taking the time to enjoy her ice cream, she gave me the space to continue.

'On the other hand,' I said, 'I am convinced that all things being separate and distinct is a ludicrous idea. All you've got to do is look at organizations for that. The history of business has been a history of fragmentation – splitting people up into departments, hierarchies, teams. Divide and conquer. Organizations were designed on Newtonian science. And now, organizations are wondering where the center is – what energy binds it all together. They're struggling with how to get some unity back.'

'Industrialization and large corporations were a major cause of our problems,' replied Heather. '"Progress" offered a material level of satisfaction which diverted us from our connection to community, nature and Spirit. So many of us so quickly ceased needing an intimate relationship with the Earth for our survival, that we lost our respect for it. There was no need to show caring and compassion for Mother Earth, no need to think through the consequences of our actions as caretakers. This lack of honoring is reflected in our cruel treatment of each other as human beings. Ever since, we've lost our ancient understanding that we are all part of the web of life and that what we do to the web we do to ourselves. We've been counting the cost of societies filled with people who do not take responsibility for the outcome of their actions. Maybe losing contact with nature sent us all to sleep. It's time to wake up.'

We walked down an avenue of seven huge oak trees and then turned back towards the exit. The afternoon sun warmed our backs, filling me with energy.

'Maybe there's a new consciousness around though,' I suggested. 'Think of all the bridging going on in the world at the moment. The influences of indigenous culture in Western fashion, music and advertising. Science is bridging into Spirituality. And now we have business bridging with shamanism! I think these are all signs that people are remembering the inter-connectedness of life.'

'I hope so. There's a ridiculous delusion of separation in our society,' Heather continued with passion. 'It's what allows us to buy ten litres of a petrol and believe that we haven't in any way affected an indigenous people somewhere, or the environment. We switch on the air conditioning and convince ourselves that we're not the ones fucking up the ozone layer. It's *them*, out there, that do that! We must learn to take responsibility for all of our actions.

'Another way we separate ourselves from each other is by thinking that our problems are unique. In my experience of helping individuals, all people share a very small number of basic difficulties – maybe even one: imbalance.'

'That's exactly like organizations, Heather,' I exclaimed. 'They're all absolutely convinced their problems are unique, and they're paranoid about letting other companies know they even have any. It's ridiculous. All these companies with the same problems, all showing a mask of perfection to each other!'

'It's arrogant and egotistical to think that we are separate,' Heather said, shaking her head. 'It gets in the way of us sharing and helping each other.'

'Have you noticed, though, that people do get interested in helping and supporting each other when things go badly wrong?' I asked, realizing this for the first time. 'You know, if there's a flood or a fire, people band together. And isn't it true that people tend to talk about their "communities" only when they're under threat, like when someone's going to build a hypermarket or a new block of offices? I wish there was a way to generate that spirit of connectedness when things were going well, without us having to be in pain before we're motivated to come together.'

We sat down for a few moments on a park bench, enjoying the late afternoon sun. A rollerblader sped by in shorts and shades, and we caught a tinny blast of the music on his Walkman.

Heather had been thinking about what I'd said.

'One of the reasons I was so attracted to the Deer Tribe,' she said, 'was because it focused on gaining enlightenment through pleasure and knowledge rather than pain. Shamanism is all about discovering and celebrating that all things are connected, are all part of a unity. It's about a connection between the emotional, physical, mental and spiritual aspects of yourself, to become whole. If you personally are in balanced unity, then you'll make clearer and cleaner connections to other people – free from need or attachment.

'And shamanism is majorly about the relationship between you and Nature, linking the physical world with the Spiritual

Realm. Within our culture, I think the major bridge that needs rebuilding is the one to Spirit. Our lives, our work and our communities have become so dispirited.'

We left the park and walked back to our cars. I could still hear those children laughing.

After our meeting, keen to learn more, I looked up 'Shamanism' on another sort of Web: the Internet.

The search engine presented the following.

Society and Culture: Religion: Shamanism
Sorcerer's Dream – dreaming, shamanism, nagualism and sorcery – personal techniques and experiences. Dance of the Deer Foundation – information on shamanic health and healing, dreams, visions and peyote. List of seminars and pilgrimages.

Health: Pharmacology: Drugs: Entheogens: Religious Use
Deoxyribonucleic Hyperdimension

Society and Culture: Religion: New Age
Alexandria Academy of Universal Metaphysics – teaching the Western mystery traditions including Gnosticism, Grail quest, hermeticism, kabbalah, shamanism.

Society and Culture: Religion: Asatru
Irminsul Aettir Asatru – a presentation of Asatru as a diverse community and related topics of interest such as Runes, Norse Shamanism (seidhr), mythology and history.

Society and Culture: Cyberculture
Topics include Terence Mckenna, Timothy Leary, Paul Watts, shamanism, John Lilly, psychological heresy, political corrections, omega point, philosophy, thought crime, an entheogenic garden and hyperspace.

Entertainment: Music: Genres: Electronica: Styles: Techno
Inner Rhythms – a journey into rave, breakbeats,

techno-shamanism, tribalism, psychedelics, technological mind expansion, and evolutionary media and communication.

Health: Alternative Medicine: Herbs
HerbWeb – Explore the Overmind through a saturated web of hyperlinks. An introduction to worldwide herbalism & shamanism.

Which clarified things as little for me as it has done for you.

Then I noticed a link to the Center for Organizational Learning. There was a review of a seminar run by a someone described as the Keeper of the Wisdom of the Iroquois tribe. I read on, intrigued. Heather was not alone then, in passing on the accumulated wisdom of ancient tradition to the business world. This woman had described how learning styles can be considered as the embodiment of certain animals: the buffalo, known for wisdom, the eagle, known for inspiration, the mouse signifying care for community, and the bear signifying introspection. How much more complete would our decisions feel, she suggested, if we considered them from all four perspectives. Wholeness incorporates diversity.

I can't help thinking, wrote the reviewer,*that if the corporate types I've known displayed this kind of sensitivity to other's needs, the corporate world might actually be a good place to work.*

Finding this web site made me certain that Heather's teachings had a great deal to say to the business world, as much as they had spoken to me personally. Yet I also realized that if I wanted to understand more about shamanism, I would have to experience it.

In particular, I wondered, how could we bring back spirit to our lives and work?

———————

I stood in the towering lobby of a client's headquarters, a place of marble walls and running water and mosaic floor. In the center, a semicircle of trees, a type of bamboo, green and powerful, leant a backdrop of softness and calm. Only meters away, the central London traffic hustled by, but this place was silent, sound-proofed, protected from the outside world.

'A great place to hold a relaxed meeting,' I commented, gazing around the lobby, as my client swiped me through the security gate and summoned the lift.

'Oh, we're far too secretive here to hold meetings in public,' she said, watching the red numbers on the display fall towards zero.

We entered the glass-walled chamber and it transported us silently upwards. As we reached the top floor, I pointed out that the tops of the lobby trees were not green in fact, but yellowing and wilted.

'They're dying,' she affirmed, shrugging her shoulders. 'It's a shame isn't it? They've tried everything to save them, all sorts of nutrients. But I'm afraid they're all going to die.'

We stepped out of the lift.

'Then again,' she concluded, 'it's hardly the place for nature, is it?'

I had driven to a country house hotel in Leicestershire to observe one of Heather's workshops: *Community in Business*. In the absence of projects from Paul and I, as we'd all originally planned, Heather had been setting up her own work. I still had an intuition that I could join her.

I booked in and asked for the conference room where Heather would be working: the Chester Hall. As I followed directions back up the gravelled driveway to the Hall, Heather's participants were arriving by coach, laughing and joking in their smart casuals.

I could hear the music even before I opened the door to the Hall – the flowing loops and curves of the theme music from the film *The Piano*. As I went in, Heather waved but did not stop as she busily rearranged furniture.

'Why do they always get this wrong?' she said, not really expecting an answer. 'It's crazy – you ask for one room arrangement and they give you another. Look at this!'

I helped Heather move all the tables to the side – some we took out altogether, leaving them on the lawn for the porters to take later. This gave Heather the room she needed to set the twenty or so chairs in a large semicircle. She closed the loop with a flip chart and a chair for herself.

Next she drew back the blinds, to reveal the most astonishing vista of trees and hills swooping down towards the horizon. It was a beautiful backdrop to whatever Heather had planned, though I hoped it wouldn't distract the participants too much.

'That's better, she said. 'Now we can all see each other! Now then ...'

She went over to a patterned carpet bag and took out first a small black, decorated pot. She unscrewed the lid and set it down on the table. I thought it was an ashtray at first, but, looking more closely, I saw that it was half full with some sort of herbs. The she took out a cardboard sheath, and pulled from it a large black and white feather.

She took a lighter from her bag and set fire to the herbs. They did not burn with flame, but smouldered enough to give off a grey smoke, smelling powerfully of sage.

She noticed the confused look on my face.

'I'm smudging the room,' she said, smiling.

'Aha!' I said. 'And that would be ...?'

'Smoke is a universal way of cleansing and purifying the environment. That's what I'm doing now. Different herbs have different properties. This is mostly sage, which Native American peoples use to cleanse and banish negativity.

'Indigenous peoples smudge as a precursor to any ceremony and use sage as an offering. It's the equivalent of the Tibetans using yak butter for their oil lamps, and the Christians offering money in the collection.'

She swept the feather in short pats at the air, encouraging the smoke to rise up and around every object. Then she walked over to me and began to waft the smoke over me, starting at my feet and working up over my head. She finished smudging me with three or four strong sweeps of the feather down my back. She seemed to put more energy into those final ones, I noted.

'I'm cleansing any remaining negative energy in your aura. The noise the feather makes is rather dramatic, don't you think?'

'Very,' I said.

'If you're going to do something, do it with energy!' she laughed.

She finished by smudging herself.

'Ideally I'd cleanse each individual as well. But when that's not possible, cleansing the space alone is still helpful. Buildings hold the energy of whatever has taken place in them. Who knows what emotional trauma might have happened in here before we came along?'

Having been present at many a traumatic company awayday, I was prepared to accept she could be right.

I took a deep breath. The smoke seemed to clear my head and wake me up.

'Why the feather?' I asked.

'Feathers are excellent energy movers,' she replied. 'The censor in a Roman Catholic Church is its equivalent. Both create the propulsion needed to move the smoke around.'

'Why don't you just blow?'

'Because when a person blows, they are transferring their own negativity onto the smudge mixture. That rather defeats the purpose. Any more questions?' she asked, encouragingly.

'Just one. Why are you doing the smudging before people arrive?'

Heather stopped what she was doing and looked at me. She had a feather in one hand and a pot of smouldering herbs in the other.

'You don't want them to think I'm weird, do you?' she said, jokingly.

That's common sense, I thought.

'Hopefully companies will soon be smudging to enhance the environment as naturally as they might turn on an air conditioner,' Heather said. 'If they find it helps, why wouldn't they? All they have to go through is the movement from non-acceptance to acceptance. I remember when ionizers were considered far out: they're pretty common now. Either the context changes and makes something acceptable or somebody has the courage to push for a new thing and make it happen – that's how things get accepted.

'A feather is only odd because it appears out of context in the business world. Perhaps an electric fan wouldn't.'

'It does the same job – but the feather's prettier.' I said.

'I agree,' she nodded, smiling. 'It's tragic how science models nature so often and then forgets the origins of its ideas. The electric fan is based on feathers and wings. Now maybe a fan works faster, or it affects a larger space – but the emphasis on efficiency misses something about the spirit of where the feather came from.

'Alchemy and metaphysics lost something important when we took the Spirit out of them and turned them into chemistry and physics. They lost the mystery and wonder of connection to Spirit – and the benefit that brings. That's what I'm trying to bring back.'

We were interrupted by one of the participants putting his head round the door.

'Ooh! Nice smell,' he said, looking around to see where it might be coming from. Heather had packed up her smudge paraphernalia by then.

He came in, smiling, greeted us both and confirmed the starting time with Heather. He went back out again.

'Well he seemed to like it!' I said.

'It's important to prepare a workshop for all five senses,' she said, nodding. 'That's why I have the music, the seating in a circle, the view of the trees and so on. I'm stimulating all the aspects – mind, emotion, body and spirit. So much business is preoccupied with mental activity. How can they expect a balanced result when they ignore three out of four aspects? We are all connected to our environment and thus to each other – so it's important to prepare our surroundings well.'

As the participants began to enter, I noticed how most of them benefited from the smudge. Many commented on the smell and, undeniably, the mood in the room felt light and open. Certainly, no-one objected; they didn't need to know the hows or whys of the practice in order to feel the benefit. What could the harm be? Only the offence given to our sense of what's normal.

The workshop began with introductions and a short presentation from the marketing director explaining the purpose of the day to the whole group. Then he passed over to Heather, who introduced herself and gave a bit about her background and how it had led to shamanic self-development being brought into the business world.

'We are going to be doing various exercises today that are designed to take you out of the place where you are most comfortable – your left brain, logical mind. The exercises will help you to experience many other ways of accessing information to assist in understanding both yourself and your company. Why? Because what you are all looking for is how to bring a sense of community to your companies. And community is a feeling, not a fact or thought. Community exists in the world of emotion and spirit, not the mind.'

I noticed some people nodding in agreement. Others, by the look on their faces, still needed convincing.

'The first exercise we'll be doing,' explained Heather, 'is known as the Flowering Tree Ceremony. The tree is – or perhaps I should say was – sacred to many, many cultures partly because trees are seen as a perfect symbol of how balanced human beings should be: with their heads – the branches and leaves – reaching up to the Spirit world – the As Above – and their feet firmly grounded like roots in the Earth – the So Below.

'The purpose of the plant kingdom is to balance the atmosphere, to bind the earth, to enhance beauty and to feed humans and animals. Plants are the great energy givers of the shamanic world. We don't own them to use and discard at will.'

As I listened to Heather speaking I realized I'd never really had a great concern for the plight of the rain forests. It seemed so far away. I did, however, think of the road protesters around Great Britain spending their lives in protecting the trees – and how they were dismissed so easily by so many as dropouts and scroungers. I remembered an interview I'd seen with one of them, when the presenter had accused this girl dropping out of society. Calmly, the girl explained, on the contrary, that she thought most of society was doing the dropping out – dropping out of our responsibilities towards the environment by focusing on a narrow life of selfishness and acquisition.

'Many cultures now honor trees for what they give us materially,' Heather continued, 'but today we're going to see if they can provide us with something less tangible. I'm going to ask you to go outside and ask one of those trees a question.'

She patiently let the hubbub die down, and revealed a series of questions about the company that she'd designed with some of the managers prior to the workshop.

She said: 'When you are talking to the tree, don't expect the tree to bend down and whisper in your ear. But be aware that information may come to you in different forms. Pay attention to any shifts of temperature, or a sudden breeze; you may notice an insect crawl on you or a bird fly overhead. Make a note of anything that happens, bring it back into the group and I'll help you interpret what you experience.

'To explain a bit further what you might experience, let me just read you this from a book by the physicist, F. David Peat:

Native people talk of speaking to animals, trees and rocks ... I think part of our difficulty may be that our society, with all the intense drama of television and film, has conditioned us to think of the voice of the rock as something that will boom and reverberate into our minds like God in a biblical spectacular.

But what if this voice is very quiet and subtle, a gentle movement unlike the normal chattering of our thoughts; something closer to a gentle breeze than a hurricane, to a sixth sense rather than a confrontation, a feeling rather than a thought, an emotion rather than a sentence? Silence surrounds Indigenous people. Could it be that the voices of trees and rocks can only be heard within such a silence? Maybe the voices are always present, but we in the West have forgotten what it is like to be still.'

I could see the mention of a scientist had made many in the room feel more at ease. If he said it, it must be all right.

'Now, at this stage,' she continued, 'people usually ask me: "Who am I talking to?" Well, to certain extent, the answer is irrelevant; it depends on your belief system as to which label you will feel comfortable with: God, Great Spirit, Allah. You may be connecting to your Higher Self or to your intuition. I can't tell you which one is true in your case. I don't know. But I do know the information you receive will be valid and valuable.

'And think of it this way if you are still in doubt. At worst you're being asked to go for a walk on a beautiful day and spend a few minutes sitting under a tree. What could be so awful about that?'

My left brain, logical voice had been throwing up objections all the way through Heather's spiel. Now it said: "Just going for a walk? What a rip-off!"

I was amazed at how much resistance I felt to this exercise, even though I considered myself a fairly adventurous and open person and I'd known Heather for some time now. Perhaps I wasn't as open to adventure as I thought.

After Heather had given the participants a simple meditation that helped answer the question 'How do I stop thinking?' I watched them file out. Heather came over. I'm sure she could see my doubts. I realized that my whole focus during her talk had not been 'what do I think?' by 'what must they think?'

'Heather this is going to sound awful, but at one point I got worried about associating myself with you,' I confessed. I was being remarkably honest. 'I was standing there thinking – "God what will they think of me?". I picked up the coffee pot at one point. I thought I might be able to persuade them I was just the waiter!'

Heather showed no sign of anger or censure. She just laughed.

'This is your thing about recognition, acceptance and approval again, isn't it?' said Heather. 'It is not important if someone else recognizes or approves of you. What is important is whether you approve of yourself. Do what you do because it brings you pleasure; if it feels right and harms no-one, go for it. In this case, I believe the participants will benefit greatly from doing this exercise. But I'd be pretty stupid to think everybody is happy about being asked to talk to trees. I'm perfectly prepared to be laughed at, as I've almost totally given my need for recognition, acceptance and approval away.'

I thought of so many business people who could not abide being laughed at. They wanted so badly to be treated with respect and solemnity. Their over-seriousness alone made them funny to me.

'I see so many people who put all their energy into pleasing others,' she continued. 'Pleasing their partner or their parents or their boss. And then, even when they've gained their approval and recognition, they're still not happy. That's because they never learned how to recognize, accept or approve of themselves.

'Now Bill. I think it's time you went and did the Flowering Tree Ceremony too, don't you think?'

Under the tree I'd chosen, I spent some moments wondering what question to ask – obviously none of the company's questions were relevant to me. Then a question popped into my head:

'Should I work with Heather in business?'

So I asked it, once repeating it in my head, and then again out loud to cover all the options. I was prepared to give it every chance to work.

And then?

Nothing.

No voice in my head. No wind blowing a leaf in my face. I opened my eyes to see if there was any visual information to find. I scanned the field that swept down to the roadside – nothing. No animals. Not even a car driving along the road.

What a waste of time! I got up, chiding myself to think that there would be anything in this. I like a lot of what Heather said, and she'd helped me personally a great deal. But this 'connecting to the Spirit world' was a step too far.

I brushed the dried grass from my trousers and turned to check nothing had dropped from my pockets.

Then my eye alighted on something – I must have been sitting on it. It was a small brown bundle of what looked like fur and dirt and bones and insect casings. Other than that, I had no idea what it was, but I decided to take it to Heather anyway.

I watched Heather take the various signals and information from the group and offer her interpretations. The group was surprised at how much of the information seemed to point to the same thing over and over again. For example, people had received many symbols that had suggested *soft*. For the rest of the morning with Heather they discussed whether this was applicable to the changes in communication style they had been curious about – to be less directive and more open to ideas from their people. There felt to be a great deal of consensus in the room over this.

As we broke for lunch, I hung back and waited for Heather to be free. I couldn't wait to test her with my little bundle.

'So what answer can you give for this then Heather? A load of shit?'

Heather looked down at the thing in my hand. Her face burst into a broad grin of amazement and pleasure.

'No,' she cried, laughing. 'It's an owl pellet!'

'Well?' I retorted, perturbed by her excitement but still convinced she couldn't pull an interpretation out of this. 'That may be so, but what has that got to do with me?'

She thought for a minute. 'It really depends what you were asking. But the first thing that comes to mind is my name.'

'Heather?' I said, sarcastically. 'Campbell? What are you going to tell me? That Campbell is a Scottish word for "owl"?'

'No, not my given name; my medicine name. It's Moon Owl.'

'Moon Owl? You mean like Black Elk or Crazy Horse?'

'Yes. Your medicine name tells you about your individual connection to Spirit. My personal power is enhanced by teachings from the owl and the moon,' she explained. She took the owl pellet from me and examined it minutely, as if it were the first she'd ever seen. 'So do you mind if I ask now what your question was?'

I paused for a while, my left brain, logical mind racing. It's a trick, I thought.

'I'll tell you later,' I said, in the end.

At the end of the workshop, Heather was given immediate feedback by a delighted Marketing Director. Others joined him in agreeing how enlightening the day had been. I could tell Heather was delighted.

On the other hand, I overheard two men talking as they left the room. I just caught one saying to the other "we could have got the same results sitting around a table with a flip chart!". Other than that I could sense no negativity or doubt.

'We don't like having our minds changed,' Heather explained as we were walking back to our cars. 'We're stubborn; any new piece of information messes up our world view, so we resist or belittle or simply ignore it. We only take in those pieces of information that continue to validate our personal mythology. If you have a dark mythology about your life, you're likely to have closed symbols that support how you see the world and you'll obey the rules and laws that keep your world in its particular box. So, for example, think back to your relationship with Paul. Your dark mythology was that he was the leader and you were the appendage. Your closed symbols were that you'd never go to a first meeting without Paul, for example, or speak first at a presentation or his name would always come first on proposals. The rules you followed supported that: Paul knows best, Paul's more talented. You only really saw and heard the information that kept you in that mind frame. And of course, the world supplied your validation, because people only wrote to Paul, or invited him first to meetings.

'That sort of mythology can take a lot of changing. The two people you overheard will have a world view that has just been challenged by their experiences in the workshop. You heard them justifying not changing by replaying their old paradigms.

'But they were in a minority, I think. Most people will try to be open – if you give them the chance.'

Later I told Heather the question that I'd asked the tree: whether I should work with her.

'But do you think we *can*? Will it work?' I asked.

'I've two answers, Bill,' she said. 'Number 1: I thought we were already working together!'

'No, no, I don't mean *that* sort of work, I don't mean working on me ...'

'And Number 2: what does "will it work?" mean?'

'I mean will it be successful? Will it make us money?'

'Bill; everything you've told me is focusing on the outcome when you know I've told you you must enjoy the journey. Who knows exactly what you're supposed to learn from an experience? There can be teachings from any part of it, not just the outcome. Even *that's* never guaranteed, because we must always honor the law of chance. Besides, the destination you're aiming for will probably have changed by the time you get there.

'The reason we're working together may not be about being successful consultants. Maybe we've met so I can help you with your marriage or your friends. Maybe we're supposed to write a book together! Who knows? If you're fixed on a single outcome you'll probably be opening yourself to disappointment.

'Even if there's no tangible, external result other than improved self-awareness, it will still have been beneficial for us to have been in this relationship. It feels right for now, it's fun, it's enlightening, it's good for both of us – that's great. Don't allow thinking about a possible, but ultimately unprovable, conclusion to devalue the experience.'

'But we have to have goals, don't we?' I asked.

Heather agreed. 'Yes; but the key is about attachment. Focus your intent on a desired outcome, set the plan – and then let go of it. Carry your plan about with you if you insist, but pin it on, don't super glue it on – so that if things change, nothing's harmed. Have you ever seen a true gambler in action? They do not, contrary to popular opinion, stand there praying and willing the horse over the line. They do their homework, plan their strategy, place the bet and then walk away. They trust to chance. That's what makes it so thrilling and magical for gamblers. So too on my path; the final part of any magical ceremony was letting go of what you wanted to happen.'

'So how would we use magic if we wanted to work together, then?' I asked her.

'We'd create a symbol, a logo – something that represented the relationship we wanted; then we'd burn it – or bury it. In ceremony you usually give away attachment to something by offering it to one of the elements. It means "we've committed to this, now it's in your hands".' She gestured upwards.

'Meaning Spirit's or God's hands? Like committing ashes to the sea for example?' I said.

'Yes, that's right. Hanging on to outcomes takes so much energy that you could be using for something else. If you are making sure that you are doing your best in the present, then you'll either bring your strategy to fruition or you'll be in the best place to adapt if circumstances change. Yet in business we make a decision and worry about it, inseparably attaching ourselves to what might happen. That depletes our energy, so that every new change leaves us weaker rather than stronger.

'This is also an ego thing,' Heather continued. 'Offering your dreams to the elements and chance shows that you understand that you are just a part of the web of life – you're not in control of it. Business might be a bit more human if it had a little more of that humility. Imagine every meeting beginning with a ritual. Some smudging at the beginning. Some moments of calm to bring everyone together. Maybe a prayer asking for help in keeping all the participants open to multiple perspectives and their emotions free flowing and evident.'

'Hey, they could all pass round the pipe of peace!' I suggested.

'But can you imagine,' she asked, ignoring my joke, 'a meeting starting with such a focus on intent and humility rather than ploughing straight into the usual battles for position? Meetings are rituals, it's just that they are devoid of the spirit and intent of ceremony. They've become routine, a habit. They drain us, or bore us, or annoy us. Business meetings need something and I know it's not more detailed agendas! Magic would come into them if each opened ourselves to other points of view and other outcomes beyond an attachment to the schedule.

'I can imagine a meeting starting like that,' she said. 'Maybe you can't.'

'Can *you* imagine a meeting starting like that?' I asked.

I was with two directors from a client, a small software house who specialized in supplying information and management systems to community trusts and healthcare organizations. I'd been advising them on redesigning their communications, and in particular their corporate presentation. I'd been telling them of the importance of opening moments and had decided, on a whim, to test out the idea of ritual and meetings.

'You know,' Brian, a big, bluff Northerner, said. 'You remind me of a meeting we had recently with one of our biggest clients – the Salvation Army. I'd never been into their offices before and I hadn't realized they began every meeting with a prayer. So they all settled down and the chief Army officer there led this little prayer for help. But it wasn't "O Hail O Most Mighty" or whatever. It was "Well Lord, we are holding a meeting to day about our new administration systems and I think we're well aware that our administration may not be too high up on your list of priorities, what with all the problems the world faces today; but we hope you grant us the patience to deliberate our decisions carefully and the good judgment to make them well." And then there was a long silence before the meeting started. I'm not a religious man, to put it mildly, so I wasn't praying; I just enjoyed the silence with them. But that silence, and those words, just seemed to put things in perspective for a moment.'

I nodded, thinking how valuable that sense of perspective might be. Any company could do this – no special language or style is necessary, only what has meaning for the individuals concerned. But is this just a desire for some quaint ceremony? No, I would expect practical benefit: balance and calmness. There would be others too, I was sure.

Then John, Brian's colleague and a much smaller, older man, added:

'I was there too, Bill. It was one of the best meetings I've ever been to. When they did that prayer, it made me drop all my usual sales pitch. I stopped being so attached to my own position and my own need to impress them. I felt like I was really with them in that meeting, rather than just a visitor, and as a result I felt that much more like really understanding them. I still got the sale, but that's not the point. For the first time in my career, I felt I was genuinely helping a client because I felt a part of them. We all became human beings around that table.'

'It was special,' agreed Brian, nodding. 'I've never experienced anything like it before or since.'

'She did *what*?' I asked.

'She taught the whole workshop using a talking stick!' said John. I was meeting a client of Heather's, trying to get an alternative perspective on how self-development helped a business. I was also testing the boundaries of 'what' she did.

For me, the mention of the talking stick immediately brought up images of old movies on TV with tepees and pipes of peace – but in this particular vision, men were sitting around in business suits and feathered headdresses.

'I'm still amazed at how she gets business people to do these strange things,' I said.

'Oh, Bill, I'm surprised at you. Business people are human beings and they share a common problem: an imbalance between talking and listening. Tell me just one aspect of an organization's life that couldn't be improved by better communication!'

John paused for a moment while he asked his PA to field any calls for the next hour.

'When we brought Heather in,' he continued, 'I honestly was expecting some advice on how to redesign our communication channels or improve the content. That's what we'd usually been helped with in the past by consultants. Heather made us realize that balanced and clear communication requires talking and listening from the heart, not the head or the ego. I tell you, it was a real awakening. I was ashamed when I saw what a manipulative, untruthful way of talking we had and how deep our inability truly to listen was.'

I remembered all that time ago when we held those first meetings with Heather in my company, with us doing all the talking.

'OK, I'm fascinated,' I confessed. 'I'll listen, you talk. What happened?'

'I'll show you,' he said. He pulled open the top drawer of his desk and took out a matt black metal stick.

'What's that?' I cried, laughing at the strange object.

I looked more closely. It was decorated with a keying embossed with John's company logo and a slot for a business card. I realized that the stick they'd created was both corporate and personal.

'The talking stick's medicine is to teach us to talk and listen,' he said.

'So you know about the concept of medicine as knowledge and understanding?' I interrupted. Why should I have been so surprised?

'Oh yes,' he went on, revolving the stick in his hands as if to examine it again for the first time. 'Traditionally, the talking stick was picked up whenever you had something very important to say and when you wanted everyone to hear and pay attention. The stick meant that you expected not to be interrupted. As a consequence of all that focus on you, you took great care to speak the truth from the heart without blame or judgment. When you'd said your piece, you would pass the talking stick to someone else for them to have their say.'

I thought that was his cue to pass it to me and so I leaned forward, reaching out.

'The powerful teaching from the talking stick is not how easy it is to talk but how difficult it is to listen,' John said. He smiled as I sat back in my chair. I realized how, even in that brief speech, I'd stopped concentrating on what he was saying and focused instead on what I wanted to do in response.

'We found it hard too, Bill,' he said, warmly. 'We realized, first of all, how usually our listening was filled up with the buzz of our own minds – denials and answers and counter arguments and rehearsals of what we might say next. All that noise, all that energy, is focused in the ego and not on the person who is speaking.'

'... not on the person who is speaking,' I repeated, trying hard to focus on every word John was saying.

'But don't go too far to the other extreme, Bill. You're listening for the intent, the meaning and the heart of what is said, not just the individual units of speech.'

John explained further:

'The next breakthrough came in seeing how much many of our conversations degenerated into shouting or scoring points or talking over each other. So the talking stick showed us what our dialogs would be like if we were more structured and less chaotic.'

'But there's always so much to say,' I said.

'I think everyone feels that,' he agreed, nodding. 'But if we're all speaking at once, what chance do we have to hear?' The excitement in his voice was audible. 'It's really made me think of what communication in business is like on a macro level. As our capacity for communication increases at an exponential rate, so the quality of communication is in danger of deteriorating. Mobile phones, e-mail, and faxes have increased the rate at which we can push and pull chunks of information around the world, but I don't think it's improving our ability to relate to people and make them feel heard. Heart to heart communication is what we're missing, to coin a phrase of Heather's.'

'What did you and your team mates make of the workshop, though? I bet not everyone has your attitude now.'

'Oh a lot of them hated it. I'm not saying I was thrilled at first. There were a whole string of lessons. We were hugely frustrated at having to wait to get our point across. We were so uncomfortable with silence that we'd try and fill in every gap, or speak before someone else had finished. We found too that a lot of what we claimed to be rational expression was in fact highly charged with what we felt – and unfortunately we were feeling a lot of dark emotions like envy or resentment or worry.'

'Wow,' I said. 'Heavy stuff.'

John accepted my comment and moved on. 'Yet the amazing thing was that Heather pushed us to discover it for ourselves. When we saw that we really were communicating like that, it was impossible to deny the effect it was having. Personally, my most powerful insight came when I realized I didn't appear to genuinely respect my colleagues' points of view.'

'Oh, John, I don't believe that.' How could anyone as open as John be closed to other people's point of view?

'No, really,' he explained, 'I said all the right things, I knew all the right games to play in influencing people. So I *sounded* like I was encouraging others' point of view. But I found that I was far too attached to my own position to give anybody else a real chance. I always had an agenda. Communication, for me, was just a head game, a way of manipulating other people to my way of seeing things. As a result, I realized, I was getting less and less back from my colleagues – fewer good ideas, fewer insights and truths.' He shook his head to himself. 'Can you blame them, though? Nobody ever felt they could make an impression on me. They knew I'd always get my way.' He looked at the stick intently. 'So I did – but I came to see that I was putting all the pressure on me to move the business forward, when what I was claiming to do was share that responsibility.'

There was a long silence. I understood the dilemma.

'But that's how you've got where you are today, John, isn't it?' I suggested. 'Have you been able to give up your attachment to your own position? Was it scary to live with not knowing what the final outcome of a conversation might be?'

John thought for a moment, and then said:

'I took my family to see the Cirque du Soleil perform last year. Have you ever seen them? God they're amazing! All that magic – and no safety net!'

He looked me in the eye.

'Do you get my meaning?' he asked, deliberately.

My time with John prompted me to reflect on my conversations with Heather. I thought how she never wasted words. Communication was a way of helping others grow, and she honored it for that. She did not take conversation lightly or for granted. Whenever she had worries and angers of her own, she would ask permission of me for the time to discuss them. Conversation was a balance too – she wanted me to be in the right place to listen, and she took care to explain if she was looking for an opinion or whether she just needed a space to understand her thoughts and feelings.

The way Heather used communication was in stark contrast to much of what I realized I experienced, especially at work. The racket of ego and display, the absolute attachment to personal position and outcome, the preeminence of logic and fact over feeling and intuition and above all the urgent rush to get one decision made so that we could move on to the next one – this was the nature of business conversation. Most interactions in my company, I began to notice, left the participants drained, even those who 'won' the argument. It was draining because it was heavily overbalanced in masculine energy – pushing out, forceful, staccato.

Maybe it was this that caused so many of my colleagues to 'recharge' their batteries in the pub – and I was like them in that. But I began to find the conversations there uncomfortable, because they brushed around the surface of so many things and gripped none of them. I noticed, on the contrary, how easily 'enjoyable chat' was able to encompass wide extremes – racism, sexism or just plain rudeness – in the name of fun. I attended one too many evenings in the pub where I'd hear the words 'Now, I'm not racist in any way' before a joke of appalling vindictiveness. This was the nature of conversation for relaxation. It was OK because we were 'off-duty'. I grew concerned that our easy distinction between what we said here and how we behaved back at the office was as false as any of the separations Heather had been talking about. Everything is connected. What we put out comes back to us.

Heather was clearly uncomfortable with 'small talk' and so rarely made it. For her, self-development was so interesting that there was no need to waste time on facile chat. This made it sound as if time with Heather was difficult and 'heavy'. On the contrary, we laughed a great deal – and most of the rest of the time I was so fascinated by what was being said and how it related to my life that the time flew by. I left Heather energized by our dialogs. Nor was it abstracted, theoretical debate. As I grew to understand the need for balance and integration, and woke up to my own imbalances and tensions, the information became a source for change in my external actions. As I took a teaching in, I would find almost invariably that, soon after, I would read about the same thing in a magazine, or see it on the TV, or I would meet someone at work who's own situation seemed applicable to what I had learned. It was as if the world offered me the chance to test the teaching, to experience it for myself.

I didn't realize I was about to be offered a teaching about the teacher.

One morning, I rang Heather early to give her news of a forthcoming client meeting. Being an owl, she preferred not to start her day before it was half over for most of us. I knew that, but, for some reason on this occasion, rang her at 8.30 in the morning.

She answered my call, listened to me for a few seconds, and then slammed the phone down. I thought I heard her say 'Fuck off' before the line went dead.

I was embarrassed at first, but thought that was my Do Gooder kicking in. Then I was appalled. I could not believe how Heather could profess to any degree of self-development and yet act in such a petty way.

'You were so grumpy!' I told her later.

'Too right I was,' she said. 'See how joyously you'd pick up the phone if I rang you at 3 am!'

I scowled. I thought she was missing the point.

'I've come down off my pedestal then Bill, have I?' she said.

I admitted she had.

'Good. I'm not an enlightened being. I'm human. Shamanism is a way of life that encompasses everything, but one thing it is not is a path of gurus. It's about self-responsibility. You mustn't follow me. Walk along side me on this path and learn what you can for your own growth. But don't treat me like a Master or guru. Expecting me – or anyone – to be perfect puts too great an expectation on me and means you're bound to be disappointed.'

'Ah well," I joked. 'We have enough gurus in business anyway.' I laughed.

'And they are just like gurus in the spiritual world. They have a truth to tell, which they have an attractively persuasive way of communicating, but they leave people dependent, not self-empowered. They take the power you are given in life to think for yourself, to make decisions based on honesty and self-awareness, to be self-responsibile. Too many people give away their power as they step into total trust and belief of the Guru's doctrine and promises. The Warrior Way is to aim for self-sufficiency, not dependency. Take your own power.'

If this was a path without a Guru, who would show me the lessons I had to learn? My mistakes, almost certainly, would be my greatest teachers. The challenge was developing the willingness to make as many mistakes as were necessary to learn. That would mean I would have to learn to forgive myself, and reduce the chatterings of my ego that only stupid people made mistakes. At the same time, I would have to increase my awareness, my capacity for noticing when a mistake was not a one-off, random event but part of a greater pattern. I would also have to develop the stability to learn from the mistakes of others, without the need to make them myself; and the compassion to observe the mistakes of others without judging the people who made them.

Mistakes were going to be a part of my life, as I suppose they had always been. But my attitude was different now.

There could be no 'failure'.

The next day, I took another step in freeing myself of my attachment to habit, safety and expectation. I needed to bring even more space into my life for magic.

I wrote a letter to my company asking them to terminate our two day a week agreement.

I leapt into the abyss.

Three days later I took a call from an old business colleague who said he needed something out of the ordinary for a workshop in Wales.

I took this as a *very* good sign.

THE EAST:
PLACE *of* SPIRIT
ILLUMINATION *and*
ENLIGHTENMENT

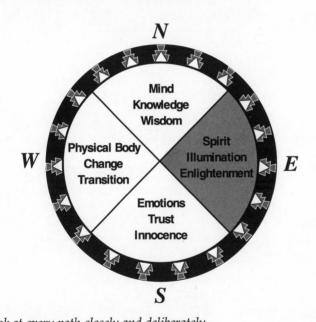

Look at every path closely and deliberately.
Try it as many times as you think necessary.
Then ask yourself and yourself alone one question.
This question is one that only a very old man asks.
My benefactor told me it once when I was young and my blood
was too vigorous for me to understand it.
Now I do understand it. I will tell you what it is:
Does this path have a heart?
If it does, the path is good.
If it doesn't, it is of no use.

Carlos Castenada

We were in Heather's car, roaring along in her 'Silver Dragon', speeding down the M4 on the way to deliver a workshop in Wales. The commuter traffic that had clung so close around us for so long had begun to dissipate as we got further from London. Eventually it seemed as though we were the only car on the road. Heather threw off the queues of traffic like old luggage, and as if released, took the car through the gears until we were cruising at well over 90 miles per hour. It was one of the signs that Shamanism was definitely the path for Heather, because unlike other spiritual ways, this one allowed her to live life to the maximum. It was the path, she'd once said, for spiritual rock and rollers.

The late summer evening displayed a blood red sky, throwing black silhouettes of far off trees onto the horizon. I saw a large, dark bird hovering over a field as we sped by. It was waiting for something to move again.

After some miles, I pulled my bag from the back seat and rummaged about for my notebook. As I was looking for the pen, I came across a bag containing a new tie I'd bought earlier that day.

'Hey, Heather, what do you think?' I asked, taking it from the bag.

My new tie was brightly colored, featuring figures that seemed to be based on Mayan cave paintings. And it was expensive. I thought it would be just Heather's cup of tea.

'Well, if I liked ties, it would be very nice ...' she said, hardly glancing down.

'Oh God!' I said, wondering where on earth she was going to take this. 'What have you got against ties?'

She threw her cigarette out of the gap at the top of her window. She closed the window, sealing the car from the outside air with a muffled *whumpf* and, at once, the quality of sound inside the car changed.

Heather said:

'The tie's a symbol. What's the single most common stereotype of the businessman, especially now that the brolly and bowler has died out? It's the tie. What can be said about all ties, whatever color or shape or design they are? That they symbolically separate the head from the body. And that's exactly what the problem is. You've heard of headless chickens – well, I think business has a lot of bodiless heads. My teachings are all based around helping business people find a connection to the body. Everything I do is based around a simple medicine wheel which I call Business Recapitation.'

I waited to let an image of bodiless heads on plinths placed around a board room table clear from my mind.

'Tell me more!' I smiled.

'OK. Draw a circle and label the four directions: North, South, East and West.'

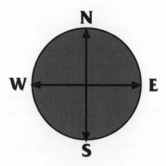

Business Recapitation

I pictured the image on the inside of the windshield in front of me.

Outside I saw the circle of the moon as a silver disc against the deepening sky.

'Then label the four human aspects that apply to each of the four directions and the four elements that correspond with each aspect. So, in the South write emotions and water, in the West write body and earth, in the North, mind and air, and, in the East, we write spirit and fire.

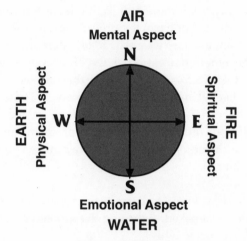

AIR
Mental Aspect
N

EARTH
Physical Aspect
W

Spiritual Aspect
FIRE
E

S
Emotional Aspect
WATER

Business Recapitation

'So already you can see what I mean by the tie. The business world is heavily overbalanced in the North, the place of the mind. As such, it cuts itself off from all the benefits that are in each of the other aspects.

'Every human problem has its root in imbalance, as does every business problem. All self-development or spiritual paths agree on one thing: that to be a fully rounded and happy human being you need to have all your aspects up and running and in the right proportions: to be balanced. It's like baking. The secret to a perfect cake lies not in having the best oven, or the freshest ingredients, or even in having the 'correct' recipe. Only by having all elements in the right order, in the right amounts, in the correct balance, will our cake be edible. This medicine wheel reminds us from time to time of some very basic and simple truths.

'Remember first that organizations are made up of people and that all organizational problems are created, exacerbated or maintained by the way people think, feel or act. So, no matter what your business problem is, it is going to be solved ultimately by changing the way those people think, feel or act.

'So this wheel gives us a way of understanding the component parts of a balanced human, before we go about trying to change anybody. As human beings, we have four aspects or energies that shape our lives: the physical – how we move our bodies; the mental – how we create ideas, memories and belief systems; the emotional aspect – the flow and ebb of our feelings; and spiritual – our focus on the unseen forces that shape our destiny, our quest for meaning. These aspects constantly interact with each other and create the complex web which is our life. Disharmony and problems arise when we favor one or more energies above the others – when the aspects are out of balance.'

'So the circle shows how to balance the aspects and what the benefits will be?' I asked, watching the moonlight illuminate the invisible medicine wheel.

'That's right,' Heather replied. 'This is the wheel I use whenever business people are seeking alignment with themselves, with each other and with their products and customers. Getting them to accept that they are probably overbalanced in head energy is not so difficult. I persuade them that any imbalance is unhealthy and will have repercussions in everything they do in their business. What is more difficult is getting them to accept one of the basic premises of all self-development work, that you most need to work in the areas you're most uncomfortable in – the bits that scare you.'

'Getting them to admit they're afraid must be a challenge in itself,' I said, after a short while.

The sky had lost almost all its banners of color and, for long stretches of the journey, only our headlights showed the way forward.

'Well that's true,' replied Heather. 'Rarely are business people intimidated by any mental construct or exercise.'

'Which is why books are so popular in business,' I agreed 'They can describe the scariest of ideas – difficult learning, fuzzy logic, chaos theory, ambiguity tolerance, empowerment, making work fun – and business people are happy to accept them intellectually. Putting the ideas into action is another thing altogether.'

Heather nodded. 'So I have to push people into facing their fears, the places where they are least comfortable – their bodies, their emotions and the world of spirit.

'Then I help them balance the aspects one axis at a time – aligning what they think with what they feel on the North/South axis and then moving onto the West/East axis: releasing spirit through working in the physical dimension.'

Suddenly I became dizzy. I noticed my vision was blurring. Perhaps I was tired. I rolled my window down a little and let the breeze blow hard onto my face. It felt good.

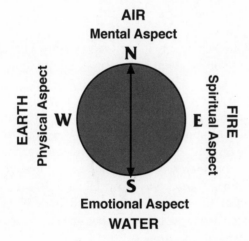

Business Recapitation

I reached out in front of me and touched the imaginary wheel at the North and South points. My fingertip left two marks on the glass. But I seemed not to be in the car any more. I was back in a meeting room somewhere. I was at work.

I said: 'I remember once working with a senior team in a big company. They were discussing their next year's strategy. It was late in the morning and the group was losing energy quickly, becoming more and more polarized and increasingly sullen. It was clear to me that the group wasn't open or honest. But no-one could have faulted the rigor of their argument or how well they had collated all the facts. But the debate was all head and no heart. It felt depressing to watch – and it was becoming clear how draining it was to them too.

'When they took a short break, one of the team joined me at the back of the room. He looked depressed. "It's crazy," he said, "We're all paid very well to create this strategy and to take it back to the company, and most of us care about getting it right, but you wouldn't guess it from the way we're talking this morning." I had to agree with him. I was sure there was much more of themselves they could give.

'As the afternoon session began, I encouraged the group to review the morning session and asked them to begin their summaries with the words "I feel ...".'

'Letting emotion come into it,' nodded Heather. I hardly heard her. The vision of the client team was still holding me.

'And do you know what?' I said, to myself as much as Heather. 'Not one of the team spoke about the contents of the strategy – they all spoke about how they were approaching the task as a team and how they were treating each other. It became clear that their discussions had a great undercurrent of emotional context that was now being released. As they tapped into this, the energy in the room changed. They became more animated as they spoke. They became concerned for each other as well as for the strategy.'

Heather said: 'When people are willing to honestly discuss what they feel, it's amazing how new points of view will open up ...' It was if her words were coming from my mouth in my vision.

'And that's exactly what happened with this group,' I continued. 'They found that sharing their feelings gave them new ideas and possibilities.

'I remember there was one moment in particular that had a dramatic impact. Many members of the team said that they felt as if they were being steamrollered by the MD and that they were frustrated. They said they felt they couldn't have a genuine commitment to the strategy since they didn't feel that they had a true share in its creation. You can imagine, Heather, that for some of them, this was a risky revelation. For once, they were telling the truth rather then "toeing the line".'

'Telling the truth from a place of balance – from the head *and* the heart – is bound to have a better result.' said Heather.

'Exactly. And they were shocked by his response – but not in the way they'd feared, thankfully. He told them that he agreed with them – he *was* steamrollering them and that he wished they would challenge him more. He wanted them to grow and was frustrated by their apparent lack of courage. That afternoon session revealed that the whole group had been living a Catch 22 situation. Aligning what they felt with what they spoke got this team out of a rut, gave them new energy and it meant that everyone committed personally to the strategy. And later we made subsequent changes to the structure and behaviors of the group which had a tremendous impact on the team's future performance.'

'All that from two little words: "I feel ..."!' laughed Heather. Her laughter broke my spell – the vision of my past clients seemed to fade.

'If only people would realize how much more difficult they make things for themselves, when they think they are making it easier,' Heather said. 'You just can't get open and honest communication if people are withholding or suppressing a part of themselves. We have been conditioned to fear and distrust emotions, particularly in business. So we withhold information about our feelings – "I'm not upset, honestly"; or we think of them as getting in the way – "don't let emotion cloud your judgment, Harry!"'

I laughed at the familiarity of Heather's examples.

'Or emotions are seen as a sign of weakness – as in "she lost control". Think of the British male with his stiff upper lip.'

'Harry's definitely one of those!' I joked.

'The way we greet people shows how we've removed the heart from business,' continued Heather. 'The common way to greet is to shake hands – we appreciate a strong handshake: it has that macho overtone to it. Think how other cultures place the emphasis elsewhere. In the East they touch their fingertips to the third eye in the forehead, the mouth then the heart, which means "that our spirits may connect, we may speak truth to each other, and our hearts may connect." There's all different versions which connect Spirit and Heart. Even if you do the French double kiss on the cheek it puts your hearts in proximity to one another.'

'So you think we should do that?'

'Not necessarily. The style of the greeting is only part of a bigger picture involving the intent behind the meeting and the behavior both during and afterwards. I'm interested by what the symbols and rituals of today's business teach us about ourselves.

'Now where was I?' she said 'Oh yes. North/South axis. Business has the problem of the North/South imbalance in an extreme form, but it comes from us all living in a world accustomed to a discrepancy between what we are thinking and what we are feeling. As a result, our words don't carry the whole truth. How often have you greeted someone effusively when your feelings are telling you how much you dislike them? We label this way of life "being polite". It's become so normal to us that we often say exactly the opposite of what we mean.

'We suppose that telling "little white lies" will be simpler than spending time going into how we really feel, but, in fact, this opposition between our thoughts and feelings has made life very complicated. It means we are putting so much energy into falsehood or "protecting someone's feelings", when the truth more often than not will help the situation.'

'That's what I could never get used to as a consultant,' I agreed. 'I've spent so long in private meetings with people who tell me just how they feel about their colleagues, their organization and about what should be happening differently, but these same people feel unable to let this "truth" come out when they are with their teammates. What a waste of their time and money! And I've never met a team which does not profess to value "open and honest communication" or "synergy". Yet those same teams only bring a part of themselves to the table. Creating a whole that's greater than the sum of its parts is hard enough without dealing in fractions!'

'Oh, very cleverly put!' laughed Heather.

The moon was fully risen now, casting its special light over the bare countryside. The road was racing by beneath the wheels of the car, but I realized I had lost all concept of how far we we had traveled towards our final destination. I looked out of my window: no landmarks, no other cars on the road, no signs of life anywhere. And no road signs. Were we even on the right road any more? Heather seemed unconcerned by such thoughts.

She continued: 'Before connecting our heart and mind with our body and spirit, we must check that each aspect is functioning at its fullest potential and in the light. An aspect that is out of balance is called dark. Self-empowerment will gradually increase as each direction is worked on and connected to the other aspects.'

'Give me an example,' I said, focusing on the medicine wheel I'd envisioned on the windshield in front of me.

'Well, having a rigid, dogmatic belief system is not going to help us when we want to change. That's the dark side of the

Mental Aspect

Dark
dogmatic, rigid opinions and points of
view, limited references
Light
open-minded. creative thinking
multiple points of view

Physical Aspect

Dark
not walking your
talk, over-emphasis
on 'macho man'
'blonde bimbo'
non-manifestation

Light:
connection to
your body,
openess to
change and
movement,
walking your talk

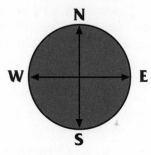

Spiritual Aspect

Dark
living the visions
of others,
without passion,
hopelessness

Light:
determined by
your inner fire,
living with passion,
illuminated

Emotional Aspect

Dark:
feelings bottled up or out of
control
Light:
free flowing expression of feelings

mental aspect. Organizations should encourage flexible thinking being open to different modes of creativity. An aspect of this is being honored for changing your mind, rather than denigrated. It takes courage to admit you've made a mistake.

'We've got to learn that it's possible to be strong without being rigid. That's why, on my path, the mental aspect is associated with the element of air – the wind blows away the cobwebs of outmoded ways of thinking.

'When we pray on my path, we ask for mirror mind, or clear mind, which is the ultimate light side of the North, to enable us to be a perfect reflection of anyone who comes to us. With clear mind, none of your own stuff – your own interpretations, beliefs or memories – get in the way. The person sees themselves reflected in you and in that way learns most about what they need to change.

'In the South, emotions are likened to water. Both feelings and water should be allowed to flow naturally, so that they don't stagnate and fester. There are many implications to this and it will take a lot of getting used to, because organizations traditionally have not been emotional places. We'll have to allow laughter as well as tears. We'll have to accept outbreaks of anger and frustration, not as signs of weakness, but as symptoms of problems that need to be heard and addressed. And as with everything I suggest, it is up to the self-responsibility of the individual to ensure they are using those emotions appropriately, in terms of timing, situation or the people involved. My path does not give us a license to turn companies into psychotherapy encounter groups!'

I gave an exaggerated shudder of disapproval and put on a whiney accent: 'Hey, guys, let's all hold hands in a quality moment and connect with our emotions here!'

We laughed.

Time passed as we moved through the dark hills of what I assumed must now be Wales. For about an hour now we had been tailing a battered blue Nissan. Then suddenly I noticed that the name of the model, spelt out in silver lettering above the rear light panel. It read SPIRIT.

Heather too seemed to be looking at something in front of her, but it was not the road. She seemed deep in thought. I didn't mention the SPIRIT car. Perhaps that's what she'd been looking at.

Eventually, she spoke again.

'We were talking about telling the truth, saying how we feel and what we think, no matter if it's out of alignment with what others think and feel. I'd hope any healthy, awake organization would encourage that. But it's got me thinking, how far can we take this? How can we be honest in business?'

'You mean, could I say to my competitor, "your product is better than mine!"?'

'Yes, that sort of thing. In my studies, I found that indigenous peoples believed honesty to be a way of life. You'd be honest to your dog. Or if you were out hunting, you wouldn't just sneak up and kill the deer. You'd do a ceremony, or say a prayer, thanking the animal for giving you its life and asking it to stand still a while longer while you loaded the arrow in your bow.

'Now, it's pretty obvious to say the world would be better if everyone lived at that level of honesty, but it's pretty unrealistic. But a good start is to question why we do what we do now. And we've got to wake up to the consequences of telling the truth or withholding the truth.

'We have this ideal that Truth is an absolute thing with its own impeccable logic. But it isn't. It's relative to the moment and the perspective – and to the person hearing it. Nor is truth-telling a left-brained activity. It's usually conditioned by hunches or intuition: by gut feeling. Think about those words: gut feeling – the physical and emotional aspects, not the mental.

'So if the Truth is so dependent on context, it's all the more reason to realize you have a serious responsibility to weigh up the outcomes, especially when your decision affects so many others.'

'In many companies,' I interjected, 'people assume that their bosses are not telling the whole truth anyway.'

'True,' said Heather, 'and, in some ways, that makes it easier to maintain deceit. Another mythology people have to justify withholding the truth is "what they don't know won't hurt them". The reality is the opposite. The truth hurts, but it usually is a short-term pain, in that truth opens us up to movement and change. It's difficult to move anywhere when you're in the dark.

'I think there's an ego thing too. People presuppose that they know how others will react to the truth, and either tell it or not in relation to that assumption. But you have to have a high level of awareness to be able to guess correctly – and it causes all sorts of difficulty when you're wrong. Why not ask the person you're talking to "Do you want the truth or the lie? How truthful would you like me to be about this?". And then the listener has to take responsibility for what they hear ...'

'But Heather, I know many managers who would say "I work in a company where there are vastly different levels of awareness or awakeness. I'd love them all to be self-responsible warriors, but, at the moment, they're not. How do I deal with the fact that most of them are going to respond in a very closed way to what they hear – they are going to want to bitch and blame and look at the negatives? What do I do?"'

'Play to the highest common denominator.' Heather said with certainty. 'Teach to the highest level and pull everyone up. Like are attracted to like; those that understand will pull together, those that don't want to hear will gradually drift away. Act in accordance with spirit rather than habit or assumption and that way you'll raise the level of your company, its awareness level and its ability to accept honesty. It may not be instantly easy to do but it's the only way to start the change. You'd be stupid to think you were saving yourself pain by making your decisions at the lowest level of people in your company, feeding them what you suppose they ought to hear.

'And don't let your choice be affected by what you think the impact of the truth is going to be. There is no way you can get around the fact that the way people react to your news is their responsibility. If someone's going to hate you for telling them the truth, or feel like shit on hearing it, they will do. People react in those two ways because they have big egos or shitty self-concepts. They need help in waking up out of that state – and you don't do it by disguising or softening the truth, or lying.'

We passed the remainder of our journey in silence. I was at turns exhilarated and terrified at the prospect of helping business wake up, to become more responsible, honorable, flexible – and less driven by its desire only to create material wealth. Business was clearly made up of human beings who had so much more to offer, who were in search of something more meaningful than the next wage packet. More and more people I met wanted to grow.

I asked one more question, the one that was haunting me the most as we approached the slate grey sea of western Wales:

'How do you wake up a whole organization?' I said.

'You don't,' she said. 'You wake up an individual, and they'll help another to wake up. It's how your baby will learn to walk – with little steps. One step leads to many. Talking up the size of the challenge you face just gives you a good excuse not to attempt it at all. Your baby won't be thinking "Shit, I'll never be able to run!"'

'My baby won't swear,' I said. 'I don't think!'

Yet the idea of bringing heart into business, balancing the North and the South of the medicine wheel, seemed scary. Moving on to the West/East axis seemed truly a leap into the abyss.

But then, I knew Heather was good at that.

≡

'So first of all I'd like you to take off your shoes and socks.'

Twenty-five business people in the grand hall of an old manor house on the western coast of Wales stared at Heather Campbell, glanced at each other and then looked, almost in unison, down at their feet. Only if Heather had said 'So first of all I'd like you to take off your trousers' could she have caused them more apparent embarrassment.

Heather took off her own shoes to show she meant business.

'In the meantime, let me give you some justification for our work today on the West/East aspect.'

Behind her, the Business Recapitation wheel was drawn up on a huge white board.

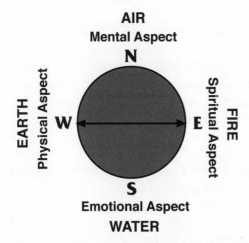

Business recapitation

'When we take exercise to relieve stress, we are making an instinctive connection between the body and the other human aspects. When we are exhausted after a hard day at the office, why do we do the seemingly illogical thing and play a game of squash? Because we know that the physical workout will bring mental refreshment and emotional calm. We will feel re-energized. Similarly, people who dance with intensity can experience heightened levels of consciousness. That's what the rave scene has all been about – the drugs have merely accelerated the process.

'Instinctively we know how the physical aspect can affect the others: how many brilliant ideas come, not at the desk, but sitting on the toilet, running for a train or brushing our teeth? These physical activities divert us from concentrating on thinking. The business world knows this too – we play golf with a business partner because changing the location and environment of a meeting helps us relax and gives us time to think. Outward Bound is the best known example. Outward Bound courses seek improvements to teamwork by putting people into physically challenging situations.

'In short, when we treat decision making as something more than just a mental, office-based, problem-solving activity, we get better at it.

'But too much of the outward bound stuff has macho overtones – it bound people together through physical fear. "Macho" is a mask and doesn't involve the heart so that we can create real change. I think it's time to soften that for the late nineties. Bravery without heart or macho leadership is not what the world needs anymore. Because we are not trying to kill the enemy in our companies; we are trying to connect together and make something that is valuable, sustaining and nourishing. We need to access that which binds people together. We are in search of unity.

'So, today we are going to try and find ways to bond together which don't involve climbing cliffs or pot holing. But that doesn't mean you won't experience fear!'

The group responded to this with some subdued laughter. They couldn't help being nervous, but weren't sure how nervous they should be.

Heather continued:

'So this workshop is about connecting to spirit through movement. And dancing is a powerful and enjoyable way of doing that. Dancing is a particularly effective tool which stills the mind, frees the spirit and releases the emotions; it is no coincidence that people have danced in all cultures since time began. There's no reason we should stop now!'

The men shuffled uncomfortably in their bare feet.

'But don't worry, this dancing is not about performance, it's about discovery. You are not dancing for anybody but yourself. There are no steps, no moves, there is no right or wrong, or good or bad. You can't fail!'

Despite this assertion, I could see what Heather meant about business people being uncomfortable with the thought of using their bodies. Some men were blushing, others pale with fear.

'It does not matter what you look like: it only matters what you feel. This way of moving is based on the Five Rhythms work of Gabrielle Roth. It's about accessing and releasing parts of yourself that have become submerged under years of conditioning, idleness, habit and fear. A lifetime of not moving very much means that we do not feel very much. Emotion is e-motion, energy in motion. We are encoded to believe we are not supposed to express ourselves, that we should not be passionate. Unfortunately that leads to unspirited people working in lifeless organizations.

'If you want the passion back in your company, the passion it had in the past, you've got to learn how to release your own passion.

'Now something else will happen today. As you release energy through movement, you'll experience the chatter of your minds quieting down. This stilling of left brain noise allows you to begin hearing insights from other parts of yourself.

'That's why you are here today. Because your left brain has not, and cannot, solve all the problems you are facing.'

There was a silence in the room, but I sensed that the participants respected what Heather was saying.

'OK,' she continued, 'first we'll do a warm up of body parts. Then I'll take you through the five rhythms of flowing, staccato, chaos, lyrical and stillness which form a Wave. Relax. Close your eyes if you want, but I'd advise keeping them open. Let go of your fear by facing it.'

Heather started the music and began the dance.

I personally did find comfort in closing my eyes at first. But as I loosened up, I glanced around.

At first, I saw what I expected to see: uncomfortable business people swaying in the constrained, disco-dancing way they probably did at weddings or company parties. But as the workshop went on, as they moved more, as they grew accustomed to the idea that they could not be wrong, they began to expand their range of movements. They swooped and dived and stretched and ran and stamped and jumped. As the time passed, I realized that the music was moving them. Their movements became spontaneous and free – they were part of the music, not a reaction to it. They were being natural. They were being themselves.

A left brain part of me said: 'But what's the practical application of this, Bill? Are you saying we should dance before every meeting?'

But that was not the point, not yet. These people were freeing themselves of their own restrictions, overcoming habit and negative self-concepts that there was a limit to what they could do. They were exploring, creating, stretching. They were facing fear and discovering something on the other side of fear. They were doing something they hadn't done yesterday – taking risks, being creative, breaking through barriers. In short, they were doing what they wanted everyone in their company to do. The dance was just a process.

At the end of the workshop, I was astonished. I could see people had been transformed. Some of them actually looked younger – I realized what rejuvenated meant. They looked so much more alive, not just because the blood and oxygen and endorphins were coursing around their bodies, but because their emotions had been released. They were impassioned. They spoke with animation about their insights, with an excitement I had rarely seen in business. The movement had brought to the fore the energies of their bodies, emotions and spirits, those aspects that our overbalanced dependence on the mind keeps asleep.

Today, people had been given a glimpse of their own potential. They had taken some of their own power back.

Above all, I saw, at a very profound level, that they had been connected to each other. The human mind, with its beliefs and ideas and opinions and perceptions, kids us that we are each different. This movement had brought all these people together in one dance and in one spirit. They had become part of something greater than any of them, something ancient, something essential. Movement is the natural state of life, utterly instinctive. Only our inhibitions keep us still.

Heather took her group through other exercises designed to release their creativity and balance, but my mind was racing.

I took a walk outside. A blue sky curved cloudlessly down to a horizon of green fields and trees. Behind me, the cliffs fell away to the sea, where gulls swooped and played in the glistening waves.

All companies begin with the spark of a new idea, I thought. Or they are driven by the passion of the people who create them. So companies must start on the the West/East axis. *Everything* is born on the West/East axis: the coming together of gut feeling and vision.

But we have no systems for maintaining that West/East balance. Organizations value above all those things which can be measured, so they shift the focus from the East and West aspects to the North. Our companies go straight to our heads.

The North – the mental aspect – is where we measure things numerically – spreadsheets, accounts, the bottom line – or verbally – in reports and mission statements. Everything in business is oriented around that measurement.

And so passion and vision is left to die. That's why vision statements are usually so unsatisfactory: words are often inadequate at summing up our feelings or intuitions. People get stuck in finding words that satisfy everyone and more often than not that sort of compromise leaves a vision statement feeling bland and passionless. Perhaps it would be better if we stopped trying to compress vision into language and used symbols and images instead. A sculpture, for example, or a painting. Anything that stirs people at a level beyond conscious, left-brained thought is going to access the spirit organizations desire.

Business keeps trying to approach vision through the head, by *thinking* its dream alive. People keep trying to get insights into where they should be going and what they should be doing; they try to recapture spirit by sitting around *talking* about it and writing it down on a flip chart. Vision is not a collection of words; it is not static. It moves. It pulses. It is energy, or spirit.

There are lots of different ways of communicating with the world of vision and passion.

Sitting around a square table under strip lighting is not one of them.

I continued my walk round the back of the manor house where the workshop was being held and found a huge, grey, abstract sculpture on a large plinth in the center of the lawn. I moved closer to get a better look, and as I strolled towards it, something in its form brought a memory flashing back to my consciousness.

I was in a client's offices, a huge building built around a central space, long and wide and with a glass ceiling open to the skies, into which the company had put a small display of sculptures. Around this central square, the sheer cliff walls of their offices rose up on all four sides.

The works of art, it transpired, were supplied by the local Art College as a way of giving coverage to the students, who were also encouraged to replace the artifacts with new ones regularly.

I asked how the organization benefited from these unusual assets.

My client looked blankly at me. 'What do you mean?' he said.

I realized that, for a moment, I didn't understand why he didn't understand.

'I mean,' I explained, 'do you find that people benefit from having this sculpture park here?'

'I think it's tax deductible,' he offered, trying to be helpful.

'No, no, I mean, do you think people are helped by being so close to pieces of art everyday. I mean, it's got to be good for their own creativity hasn't it?'

I was getting nothing back. I tried again.

'Do you think people are inspired at all by the beauty and artistry?'

'I've never thought about it,' he said, flatly.

'Well,' I suggested, trying a slightly different tack, 'it's a great meeting place. I notice that there are chairs and benches around. I imagine this place can get a bit like the old market square, you know, lots of chance meetings, spontaneity, chat and the like. A place for community to happen.'

He looked at the benches as if for the first time.

'Do you encourage people to use the space in that way?' I asked, with a hint of impatience in my voice.

For the first time, my client became animated. He made a sucking noise, taking a sharp intake of breath through his lips, denoting both surprise and denial.

'Gosh, no.' he said, pointing out through the glass walls to a row of box like rooms beyond. Each of them had the blinds closed. 'Those are the official meeting rooms.'

I nodded. 'Yes, I see that now.'

We moved towards the exit to take up occupancy of one of the rooms, to close the blinds, and begin our own meeting.

Just before he closed the door to the sculpture space behind us, he gestured up at the glass roof towering five stories above us. Through the glass I could see white clouds gather and move in the fresh wind.

My client was looking upwards too.

'Really,' he said, shaking his head, pointing and moving his hand up and down. 'Look at all that wasted space.'

Back in Wales and in the present day, I joined the group in the manor house.

Heather was bringing the workshop to a close by talking about a concept she'd mentioned at the beginning: masculine and feminie energy.

'Every human being is composed of 50% masculine and 50% feminine energy,' she said, '– although I emphasize that this is not about gender. The most common representation of what I mean is the yin and yang symbol, where a whole circle is made from the combination of opposite shapes and colors.

'Most men tend to be overbalanced in masculine energy and most women in feminine energy, but this is not not an infallible rule. I personally have always been able to work more easily in masculine energy. It's not about good and bad

or positive and negative. We are not seeking to eliminate one or the other here – we are trying to develop and balance them. As with all things, problems arise with imbalance.

'So what *do* we mean? Masculine energy is active and conceptive energy – the going out and doing energy. That's what you felt in staccato. Feminine energy is receptive and creative – bringing something into the self and transforming, creating something else. That's the flowing rhythm of your dance. Only when you combine both those energies is it possible to give birth to something. Take the most natural metaphor – a child is conceived through the combination of the male entering into the female and giving something in the form of sperm. At the same time, the female receives it and combines, transforms it into the new life. In the pregnancy itself, the woman needs both male and female energy – the period of growth and development inside the womb is ended by the great burst of male energy as she pushes the baby out. But every new thing we do or try to do involves birthing. Your dream of a new job, your hope to move house, the launch of a new project, in fact any new beginning – all these require a balance of receptive, creative energy to nurture the dream, and active, conceptive energy to go out and make it happen.

'Traditionally, people have looked for in a partner the energy they most lack themselves – from which we get the stereotype of the woman staying at home and the man going out to bring home the wage. However, that means each person is incomplete without the other. We should be aiming to find the balance of both these energies in ourselves, so that we become whole and independent.

'Women looking for independence have traditionally done so by trying to emulate men – since ours has been a male-dominated society. Whether it's burning bras and short hair in the sixties or the power suits of the eighties, women have sought to become successful by suppressing their femininity and acted in the hard, tough manner associated with men – Margaret Thatcher for example. There are many men who have lost their virility by overbalancing in feminine energy, of course. Being a macho man is just as limiting as being a blonde bimbo, but so is being a man without any fire or passion or sexual energy. Unfortunately, there are few role models of either sex who are working from a balance of both energies.'

Heather gestured to the drawing of the yin/yang again, following its contours and design with her hand.

'If we are to empower ourselves, we all need to develop our weak areas, those we have most difficulty with in order to step into balance.

'Business needs both masculine and feminine energy to give birth to its dreams. It has traditionally favored the male energies of logic, analysis and the word. The macho way we "work until we drop" encapsulates the hard masculine energy that business is usually conducted in. But living in such imbalance produces stress and exhaustion. It also denies the receptive creativity, the hunches and intuitions and the powers of image and symbol which are associated with feminine energy. Masculine energy can manage a project, but it does not have the openness to make the people in that project feel embraced as part of the whole. It drives, but it does not nurture.

'Ironically,' Heather concluded, 'it is the masculine energy way in which business thinks that makes it so difficult to change. The "mind" of business is hard, logical and forceful – it confines its focus to what it considers to be concrete, practical reality. If it could open to the receptivity, openness and creativity of feminine energy, the business world would discover new perspectives and practices. It would have spirit.

'So to change business, to create a reality that combines control with freedom, toughness with compassion, logic with creativity, staccato with flowing, each of us needs to work on balancing these two energies.'

That night I dreamt ...

... I was standing in a circle drawn out with marker stones and candles. I felt I had come a long way to be here. There was also a sense of completeness: the South, the place of trust and innocence, the place of water and emotions; the West, the place of the physical body, the place of earth and change and transition; the North, the place of the mind, the place of air and knowledge and wisdom; the East, the place of Spirit, the place of fire and Illumination and Enlightenment. Four directions. Four human aspects. Four elements. Four manifestations of energy.

I was at the center of the circle where the two axes intersected. I could sense energy pulsing from each direction towards me. Each of the four paths, I knew, was a journey into the center of me, where I could make contact with a Higher Self for insight and understanding. But the energy also pulsed outwards, back to the real world. This journey was a way of life, a way of action. It was grounded in reality.

Then in my dream the wheel suddenly began to shift and move. It expanded around me until I was completely encased in a sphere. Surprised, I put my arms and legs out to steady myself. I was wedged, perfectly balanced, against the walls of the sphere, for all the world like a Da Vinci drawing. The sphere revolved in its universe.

But then the whole mood of the dream changed. The sphere revolved, but somehow moved inside out as well as upside down, leaving me twisted and buckled. The place – wherever I was – was darkening, a chill beginning in my guts. My heart was bursting with all types of emotions that could not seem to be released, my head racing with thought after thought, playing uselessly at high speed through my mind.

And then I became very scared, because I felt my heart jump and flutter and then thud, thud, thud, just as it had done all those months ago. I could feel that everything that had been right was now wrong, shifted, transferred.

———

'What did the dream mean, Heather?' I asked her the next day. 'I was so content in the sphere – I felt that it meant I'd finally understood what each direction could teach me. But why did it all go wrong?'

'Perhaps the dream was teaching you that understanding each direction in itself is only the first step.'

'What do you mean?'

'The key is how you use the energy in each direction,' she said. 'Give with the Emotions, Hold with the Body, Receive with the Mind and Determine with Spirit. That's using the four energies in their appropriate manner.

'We tend not to do that however. For example: we habitually hold with the emotions and give with the body. Think what that does to our health and balance. By keeping our feelings locked up we think we'll be safe; so we hold our emotions in, and that results in ruined relationships and heart attacks.

'We give with the body by doing things for others instead of being there emotionally for them. The mother slaving over a hot stove is a perfect example of the transference that occurs between actions and feelings.

'Then we receive with the spirit and determine with our minds, making decisions by logically working things out and pretending to have total control of the outcomes. It's the difference between following the letter and the spirit of the law. We can justify all our actions using reason – logic's good at that – but are they the right actions and would Spirit have suggested a better way forward if we'd listened?'

———

I met a Director with one of the major Information Management companies. In his large corner office we stood at his window looking down over the car park, through which streams of employees passed on their way to lunch.

Over our own lunch, we'd been talking about ideas that have transformed business.

'Hey Bill!' he said suddenly in mock enthusiasm. 'I've had this *really* great idea! Instead of getting people to grow a great business, why don't we get a business to grow great people?'

He smiled sarcastically at me, although his irony was not directed at me, and shook his head.

'You're sounding disillusioned,' I suggested.

He pursed his lips and shook his head. 'No. On the contrary. I've made a decision, Bill.'

'Go on,' I said.

'I don't want teams anymore,' he said to me, with feeling in his voice. 'I want a community. And I want to change my relationship to everybody. I know service and support releases more energy than command and control.'

'What's wrong with your teams?' I asked, surprised at his statement. 'They achieve, don't they?'

'I'm not saying that they don't get things done. But they're one of the symptoms of what's flawed in our thinking about business. What do teams stand for in most people's minds? Competition! Winners and losers. Or they're associated with goals and targets. Or with transition – teams form to fix a problem, win and then break up. Well, I don't just want us to compete, I want us to collaborate; I don't just want us to have goals, I want us to have a shared purpose; and I want something more permanent than the next hot issue. Where's the sense of community, of service and support in all that?

Where's the caring? Nobody thinks of the greater good when you're hell bent on winning the cup.'

'You sound more of an idealist than I am, Chris.'

'Is it a problem if I am?'

'No,' I said, smiling, 'I'm just not that used to it.'

Chris opened his mouth as if to say something, but then shrugged his shoulders.

'Most people would envy your group's success,' I reminded him.

'I know. I mean, why am I even talking with you, Bill?' he said. 'Why should I need a consultant?' He gestured over to a series of graph printouts recently attached to his wall. 'Look at the revenue figures. Look at the ROI. Do you want to talk about profitability? We're one and a half times over target. Or growth? We can't keep the business from walking in through the door and we almost can't recruit fast enough to deal with all the work.'

He spoke with vehemence: 'Success? We have success!'

Then he turned to look me in the face, moving his hand between us as if to grasp at something elusive.

'But, you know what, Bill? There's something missing in this company and success isn't filling the void ...'

A silence fell between us.

'How do you know?' I said at last.

'Hah!' Chris shouted. 'That I can answer!'

He gave me a big smile: 'You see, I *don't* know.'

He sounded almost proud.

'I don't *know*,' he said, 'but I can sense it. It's a feeling, a hunch. It's in my body, not my head. What I'm looking for isn't carried around in people's minds. It's in their hearts.'

Chris turned away from the window and walked back over to his desk. He adjusted a calendar and a photo of his wife.

'Do you ever think you're mad, talking in this way?' I asked, keen to know the answer, since he was sounding as much like me as I did. 'Or do you consider all this dangerous talk for a "normal" business?'

'No,' he said slowly, staring at the photo. 'I just know I'm right. And besides,' he added, glancing again at the charts on the wall, 'there's nothing normal about excluding something just because you can't put it on a graph.'

I laughed. 'I agree,' I nodded, though it hardly needed saying.

Chris had picked up the photo of his wife.

'You know,' he said, sadder now, 'I have experienced the limitations of measurement and analysis.' He held the photo for me to see. A beautiful woman smiled from it; I could see beneath her face some sort of message, a signature in black ink, and a date which was now some ten years passed. 'It's not always the most useful thing in the world to be a good project manager,' he said.

I looked away from the photo back out of the window at Chris' colleagues, coming and going to and from their workplace.

'Don't worry, Chris,' I said. 'You're not alone. I think you're already part of a community.'

Summer was here, and with it an opportunity to take some time to visit family in Arizona. Only as I was leaving did I realize that Arizona was also the place Heather had done most of her studying.

'Can I bring you anything back?' I said to her at the end of our last workshop together before my holiday began.

Heather was replacing her smudging feather in its cardboard sheath.

'If you find something suitable, yes, that would be lovely,' she replied. 'You'll know what it is when you find it.'

'And is there anything I should be looking for out there?' I asked.

'Yes there is,' she said quickly, with a sudden certainty which made me think she'd been expecting my question. 'Search for something sacred.'

On the third day of our holiday, Grace's family and I took a drive to Phoenix, crossing the hot plains, and stopped for gas in a small town who's name I missed. It could have been Anywhere – motels, a bar, a Taco Bell. Being in the South West, its main source of trade was passing tourists. The main street had four different stores offering *Authentic Indian Jewelry and Crafts*.

I went in the first one.

One glance around the place confirmed my intuition – that the word authentic was being used in a very liberal sense. Every shelf and every display case was full of imitation junk. Nothing struck me as having any real energy or power; nothing felt right.

There were two other people in the store – a middle-aged woman with heavy makeup and recent hairdo behind the counter – and an old guy sitting on a stool nearby. My attention was drawn to the man. He must have been well over seventy, his face was heavily lined and creased with age. His skin had that buff, leathery quality from long exposure to the dry heat of the desert sun and which was all the more set off by the shock of silver hair on his head. He was wearing a denim shirt and jeans, black boots and a rodeo tie.

'Load of junk, eh son?' he called across the shop. He can't have failed to notice the speed at which I was moving past each display.

'Walt!' snapped the woman. 'Mind your tongue! If you can't say anything helpful, don't say anything at all!'

Walt laughed, a gruff, throaty laugh that caused his shoulders to move up and down. He looked over and winked at me.

'I tell the truth,' said Walt turning to the scowling woman. Then he looked again at me. 'The truth may hurt in the short term ...' He laughed his dry, low laugh again.

I recognized Heather's words. It was a shock to hear them coming from this old stranger in some town in the middle of nowhere. I was a little confused by them, and found myself musing in the middle of the store, not looking at any display in particular. Should I stay or leave? If I stay, I thought, I may have to speak to these two.

'It makes you think what we did to them.' said Walt, still looking at me.

'To who?' asked the woman.

'The Indians, Margie,' he explained. 'We stole their land, we killed their buffalo – hell, killed most of them – and then rounded up the Indians that were left and put them on the reservations. And now we're dishonoring their crafts and art with this rubbish.'

'Walt!'

'I've seen a reservation on TV,' I said, trying to save the woman from any further embarrassment. 'They look pretty grim.'

'We gave them the worst of the land and not much of it,' said Walt.

'It's what they deserve,' said Margie. 'Drunks!'

'Wouldn't you drink,' he said, pointing at her, 'if you found it difficult to forget how much you'd lost? No work, no honor, nothing to look forward to but the government taking back more of the scraps of the land they'd given you – because now they've found something else they want: the minerals on it. Yes, you'd drink.'

I made a move to leave. I was embarrassed to have got caught up in an argument that I knew little about and which was not mine. The woman smiled a polite storekeeper's smile, calling 'Come Again!' as I left.

Walking into the heat outside was like walking into a sauna: it met you as you moved.

I glanced at the town hall clock and calculated I had about twenty minutes before meeting my family back at the car. I crossed the road ordered a beer in *Mike's Lounge*.

On only the second swallow from the ice cold bottle, I was aware that Walt was sitting right beside me at the bar. I was astonished that he could have moved so quickly to catch me up. We exchanged no pleasantries or greetings because Walt launched straight into the conversation, taking up where he'd left off in Margie's store.

'But the main thing that you're worrying about,' he said, 'is not whether you can sympathize with the Indian's plight. You're not concerned about that because you're a nice guy, you've a big heart.'

I looked at him quizzically.

'No, what you're asking yourself "If the Indian culture is in such a wreckage nowadays, why should I bother listening to what they have to teach?"'

He was absolutely right. Why follow teachings that had apparently so absolutely failed the teachers? Their medicine wheels hadn't prevented them from being overrun, abused and shamed.

But how did he know of my interest in the first place?

'You're missing something in your life and you're searching for whatever it is that'll make you feel whole. You're not alone in that. Heck, you're me twenty years ago.'

'Why?'

He looked into my eyes. 'I made my fortune as a trader on the money markets in New York back in the sixties. Walked away. Up and left. We were just highly paid stress eaters, working harder and harder and buying up more to compete with the next guy. I realized in the end that deep down everyone was scared.'

'Why were you scared if you were so successful?' I asked.

'Scared that if this was all there was to life, then we'd already done it. Or scared that we might be missing something else. Scared of being lonely, maybe: *infinite riches in a little room*. Doesn't matter. The details may be different, but the story's always the same.'

He gazed up at the TV where a baseball pitcher, with exaggerated drama, pulled his cap low down over his eyes. Walt finished his beer and put the bottle down on the bar, sliding it away towards the barman.

'Personally, I think I just forgot why I was doing what I was doing,' he continued. 'So I came back here, which was home for me anyway. I'd had enough of competing with others. I wanted some space to compete with myself for change.'

'What do you mean?'

'I've always enjoyed connecting with people. Making friends. Spending time with family. The first thing I learnt from the world of business is that competition separates people rather than connects. In order to compete with something you have to detach yourself from it. If you're detached, you compare. If you compare, you judge. If you want to live a life comparing yourself to others, go ahead. It might even work for you if you always win. But what happens if your competitor wins? How are you going to feel when you've always depended for your sense of self-worth on other people not doing as well as you?'

I put my hand up to stop him.

'You haven't heard of the Deer Tribe, have you?' I asked.

'Who?'

'Never mind,' I said. 'You were just reminding me of someone I know.'

Walt looked at me strangely.

'As I say – I saw people thrive on competing,' he continued, 'because they wanted to be the top of the pile. What I saw was that the more they tried to rise above the rest, the more they were dependent on the rest to play their part in coming second. The more they tried to separate, the more they were attached. They could only define themselves in comparison with others. It was madness, self-delusion.'

'But you said you wanted to compete with yourself.'

'Because you don't have to worry about how anyone else is getting on,' Walt affirmed. 'The competition lies in always improving what you do and the manner in which you do it, so that you increase your own self-worth.'

'And have you found what you were searching for?' I asked, paying for the beer he'd ordered himself.

'Maybe, maybe not,' he said. 'I don't think I'll ever stopping looking.'

I understood what he meant.

He took another drink from his beer and changed the subject:

'The fact that many Indians lost their way and don't follow their old teachings is not really any different from a man calling himself a Christian and not living in the way Christ taught. Besides, the Indians had most everything that was good knocked out of them, either through war, disease or the abuse and ridicule that the White man brought. If they need it, they've got a pretty good excuse for not caring any more.

'But many of them still do care. And some of them are carrying on the old oral tradition of keeping the ancient medicine alive. Many cultures, not just the Native American, predict that we are on the verge of an age of harmony and spiritual awakening. There's a Hindu myth, for example, which says that we are currently in the last great age, when all the teachings of the past ages will be made available to all people, but most of them won't be interested in hearing it.'

'You seem to know a lot about this,' I said.

Walt laughed. 'Well, I studied cultural anthropology when I was younger ...'

I was amazed at another coincidence – that had been Heather's degree. 'Where did you study?' I asked, holding on to the bar in case he said 'Brown University'.

'Berkeley,' he responded. 'I've always had a great pull towards the Indian though. They'd work on my father's farm when I was a boy. I learnt a lot direct from them then.'

'Why do you think the White man dismissed so much of the Native teachings so viciously?' I asked. 'What did they have that scared us so much?'

'They had a cosmology,' he replied, '– a relationship to the earth and the animals and the universe. That didn't exactly scare us in itself; it's just that we had different priorities then. We had guns, whiskey, a hunger for money and a great ability to deceive, and it was easy for us to dismiss them as primitive and savage. We thought we were bringing them what they needed, since, in our arrogance, we couldn't believe anyone would want to live in any way other but ours.

'Of course, the irony,' Walt said, 'is that we could do with just such a cosmology now, given what our way of life is doing to the planet!'

I looked at the clock hanging over the door. I was late already.

'Walt,' I explained, 'look, it's been a pleasure talking with you, but I've got to go – my family are waiting.'

I was truly sad at having to leave.

'Hey, that's no problem!' said Walt. He swallowed down the last of the beer and got up from his stool, offering me his hand to shake.

'I wish you well in your search,' he said, genuinely. 'Oh, before you go ...'

He picked up a beer mat from the container on the bar in front of him, tore its printed cover from the cardboard, and used the resulting white space to jot something down. When he finished, he passed it over to me.

'One of the old Natives who used to work on our farm told me this when I was young. It might help you at some point.'

'Thanks,' I said, putting the card in my shirt pocket. 'I've enjoyed meeting you.'

I shook his hand again and left.

Later that night, having returned to our motel, and leaving the family relaxing in the lounge after dinner, I spent some time alone in my room.

I thought back over my extraordinary meeting with Walt, remembering what Heather had told me about synchronicity and resolving not to be so surprised at how or why I'd met this old man in a desert town. But what had it taught me?

Lying on my bed, I pulled the beer mat from my pocket and read it for the first time. On it, in Walt's firm script, was written just one line:

EVERYTHING IS SACRED

I remembered immediately Heather's advice on what to I search for in Arizona ...

I thought I might have been looking for something very old (the word 'sacred' had that sense of time passed) or for some icon or object of mystery and power. And now I was being told that not one thing was sacred, nor just a few things, but *everything*.

This was patently not the case. Some things, yes, granted. The mystery of life itself, yes. Love, perhaps. But not everything. I had only to think of that one subject I knew most about. How could anyone suggest that business might be sacred?

I was surprised at how quickly I disproved the ridiculous assertion. Alone in a little room thousands of miles from 'work', my head filled with images of the business world.

Look, I thought to myself, *at what we've made of business so far.*

Can it really be that we spend the majority of our waking hours engaged in activity which we would not do if we believed we had the choice? *The Great Escape of the Lottery hovers behind our work lives, promising to free us, if only it could be us. And the consequence is that our spirit is suffocated between delusions of imprisonment and fantasies of freedom.*

And we work increasingly prolonged hours, without sufficient time for renewal or recreation, in buildings designed for efficiency rather than effectiveness, that are bland and deadening. And we sit in the car/train/bus on the way in and we sit at our desks all day, tension hardening in the neck and shoulders. And the consequence is that our bodies grow rigid and unyielding against the turbulence of busy-ness.

And whilst we work, we engage in alliances with people whom we would not choose voluntarily to be with. Our associations with people with whom we spend at least as much time as our families are often free of the love, patience, respect and mutuality that marks a truly caring and sustaining relationship. And the consequence is that our hearts are starved of the nourishment which comes from intimacy with others.

And we perform within cultures with their own powerful rules and laws, both written and unwritten, in which we are complicit and unquestioning. So we offer ourselves up to an impersonal bureaucracy that defies our influence and distributes power with gross inequity. We accept and legitimize the powers of managers whom we neither elect nor can hold accountable. We continue to justify all business decisions with the demands of profit-making, the financial bottom line. And we are arrogant enough to assume that these decisions, overbalanced in the head and unheeding of the calls of the heart, fully discharge our responsibility to all our stakeholders – our staff, our customers, our environment, as well as our own souls. And the consequence is that our minds lose their curiosity and creativity, since devout obedience requires no thought.

This is not sacred business.

I was surprised at how disillusioned I seemed to have become with the world of organizations. But was this a balanced view?

I took a moment to breathe deep, attempting to release the tension that had settled into my shoulders and neck. As my body adjusted, the bitterness I'd felt began to subside.

Then I read the card again. This time, the single line that Walt had written seemed to set my mind racing, thoughts tumbling from my memory, drawing strands of understanding together.

I realized there could be ways to change my dark dismissal of business around.

A sacred business would be created around people who choose to be there, so that their spirits are free. Those people would give themselves the time to create caring relationships, so that their hearts are nurtured. They would have the space and opportunity to move, so that their bodies are flexible and healthy. Their minds would be fresh and imaginative, since thought would be focused on creating the future and being in the present rather than reproducing yesterday. And people, in all their diversity, would be aligned together behind a collective identity and purpose which they helped create.

And this balance, and with it all the consequent demands on the individual for self-responsibility, would be a prime concern or focus of the business, not a secondary value or background hope. As such, it would be given all the necessary resources that any core business activity or project would expect.

Is this the community beyond 'teams' that my client Chris was seeking?

The sacred business would demonstrate clearly that the learning, growth and happiness of its people were a prime objective. Leaving the organization, for example, would be a less painful operation. It would be a cause for celebration in a company to know that someone had outgrown them. The individual will end up happier, after all, and the company will end up with someone who wants their job more. It would be a strong sign of the sacred in a business: that it could love someone enough to set them free.

In my room in Arizona, I sang the chorus from the song out loud.

Sting knows this. Surely it's not too much to ask that we learn it too?

I smiled.

Perhaps this vision of business being conducted around the central principle of human growth leading to financial growth (instead of the tenuously 'real' opposite), would be frightening to accomplish. It would be a leap into the abyss.

It is frightening to do something that we have never done before, or to transform the task at hand by doing it in a completely different way.

Central shamanic principle: face your fear. Don't ask for your fear to be made more safe and palatable.

Working through fear and coming through to the other side leaves us exhilarated, not damaged. An organization of people who are accomplishing those personal victories would generate a positive spiral of courage and achievement for all.

I spun round off the bed and stood up.

Having grown this dream in the womb of the West, in the place of feminine energy, how do we give birth to it?

I paced the room.

How do we use our fiery masculine energy to manifest our vision into a new reality? Where do we start? Draw up a plan? Wait for someone else to come along and give us the plan?

What can each person do for themselves?

I looked out of the window at the distant desert plains in the warmth of the early evening light. Closer to my view, the streets were busy with traffic and neon signs. A road sign showed two routes converging.

We can start by considering the responses we make to the choices we are given.

Ours is a society driven by the word 'yes'. Our organizations create an apparently inexhaustible variety of consumables, stimulating our individual desire to be better, faster, more informed, differentiated, personalized. Our consumption of these products leaves us not satisfied, however, only more ingenious in demanding something new to replace them. It is as if we have lost the ability to say 'no', or even 'perhaps'. These are words we will have to become more comfortable with, as we adopt a responsible consideration for tomorrow. We will create the future by choosing to say 'no' just as surely as we have created our current reality by saying 'yes'.

Nobody would argue, for example, that our current experience is one of constant change. Indeed, the changes now appear to be coming so thick and fast that we are constantly surprised, shocked and exhilarated by them. Everyone appears to be rushed, up against it, stressed, ragged, running fast just to stand still.

We will only begin to create a different future for our children if we realize that it was we who created our present. For the past twenty years, speed has been the key to success and power. We've worshipped it. Then we gave it to millions of talented people around the globe, all using it to generate other ideas, processes and products. Speed, the benefit we wanted, pulsed out into the web of life and came back to us, but in a form and as an experience we would probably not have chosen. Thinking that if we worked faster we would be able to give ourselves the time to relax at leisure, we forgot the old adage that work expands to fill the time available. Rather than setting us free, speed has left us trapped.

Saying 'no' means understanding the long term as well as the short; the bigger picture as well as the immediate challenge; the seventh generation as well as our own, in the Cherokee way; using the eyes of the eagle, in Heather's words, as well as the eyes of the mouse.

The only place to start is with yourself. Becoming able to say 'no' to what you no longer want in your life is not simply an act of willpower or discipline. It means exploring the dark side of your self, the parts of your conditioning that have made you say 'yes' to whatever was offered you in the past.

Creating a better future needs idealism and imagination; it also takes self-discovery. This balance is called dreaming awake: it is not an easy task.

Blind progress, on the other hand, is much, much easier.

Driving back to the airport at the end of our holidays, we stopped at a picnic spot on the main highway. A couple from Minnesota were already there, making sandwiches. I left my family talking with the couple, enjoying the shade, and walked out into the desert. I found myself in front of a Joshua Tree. I decided to find out if there was anything else I could learn, something maybe that would back up the insights I'd been given of the old Indian via Walt.

I took a moment to relax and then asked if the tree could tell me what the business world needed to do.

Two things came to me at once. My attention was up close to the tree, examining every twist and turn of each branch, the hair-like strands of wood falling this way and that. This vision said to me: *confusion*. Then I noticed, right in front of my eyes, a new shoot of a branch, as yet only tiny, but very green and fresh against the dust-covered age of the ancient tree. And this said to me: *new growth through resurrection*.

Then I knew what the business world needed to do. There *is* a lot of confusion about: these *are* difficult times. But this can be seen in a positive light, in that major change forces people to question whether the ways things have always been done are necessary or sensible for the future. Confusion leads to questioning, which in turn awakens us to the possibility of choice.

We have a choice, always, to take a simpler, if not necessarily easier, way. And fresh shoots of understanding are growing from the depths of an ancient wisdom.

When the wind blew up and took me out of my daydream, I realized I was hungry. I walked back over to the picnic area and ate lunch with my family.

Landing back home two weeks later, summer has not come to England.

I notice as I haven't noticed before how easily the mood of the country is dependent on external things. A new Government sweeps into power with a heady majority, bringing an exhilarating sense of rebirth and possibility to the population. Building society flotations put big chunks of cash into people's pockets, and a sense of shared financial wellbeing pulses across the land for the first time in years. We've got a new, young Prime Minister and we're feeling rich: times were never as good. So when our national cricket team wins the First Test Match against an ostensibly superior Australian side, the mood of elation and pride and optimism is almost palpable. Surely it cannot last?

It doesn't. Over the next months the sun steadfastly refuses to come out, and the rain makes a mockery of Wimbledon and the Second Test. By the time, our boys lose the Third Test, the meteorologists record the second wettest June of all time and the Bank of England announces an interest rate rise, things are just about back to normal. The mood of possibility recedes.

This has been an extraordinary last few months, but for me only confirmation that if one of our freedoms is the pursuit of happiness, we should not be dependent for that happiness anywhere but in ourselves. Moods come and go, but true happiness, based on self-worth and self-competition, is more stable.

I duck out of the rain and kill thirty minutes before a business appointment browsing a book store in the City. I decide to look at the latest business book releases and climb the stairs to find the relevant shelves.

Immediately I notice that the business section is placed directly next to a section labelled *Mind, Body, Spirit*. I spend long moments staring at the two adjacent headings.

BUSINESS   MIND, BODY, SPIRIT

I smile to myself. It's good to see that even the book shops have joined the community.

Then I'm overwhelmed by the need to bring these two categories into one. So much of our lives – how many years, how many days? – is taken up in work. Surely we can use that time not as a transaction – a trade-off of my time for your money – but as an *investment*. These are the years of our vital maturity. If we can't learn to develop and grow at work, to discover our potential amidst constant change, to explore mind, emotion, body and spirit, when else will we find the time?

On the way back out, I glance at the magazine section and notice two magazines at either end of the main display. One is called *Spirit*. The other is called *Stuff*. The one is aimed at people who believe satisfaction is to be found through the soul in its connection to all life. The other preaches the message that happiness comes in the form of accumulated possessions, and offers advice on which are the best, coolest and hippest goods to buy.

I fight an urge to go into judgment. It is easy to say one magazine has got it right, the other wrong, but I know there is something more to it than that. A year ago, there would not have been the demand for a publication called *Spirit*. That in itself is a sign of something: a new approach to life, a search for something enriching and meaningful, shared by more and more people. Then again, I realize, a year ago there would not have been the demand for a publication called *Stuff*. What is that a sign of?

The aim is balance, I can hear Heather say, because that's how the whole universe vibrates – always seeking equilibrium. For every action there is an equal and opposite reaction. For every move towards spirit, there'll be a counter-move that pushes people towards stuff.

Every step towards the light makes you more aware of the dark.

On Monday nights, Heather holds a Roth5Rhythms™ dance session in a village hall in a Surrey village.

A small group of us gather to dance. For some it's a journey. For others it's an exercise. For me it's both.

Heather says to newcomers that it's not a class, as she doesn't teach it. This is her way of making sure that at least once a week she gets to surrender to the dance for herself. On another level, by saying that, she's reminding me that we can only ever teach ourselves.

On Monday nights, we gather in the lobby and carry the CD player and Heather's bag of music into the hall. There's a group of people doing karate. I always watch with admiration. Masculine energy; hard, forceful, thrusting and beautifully disciplined. They do their dances too, choreographing patterns and movements into the kata they have to display in order to demonstrate their development. They always finish with press ups, on the knuckles rather than the flat hands. The sensei counts to 20 or beyond in Japanese, but most of them have collapsed into exhausted laughter before he gets there. It's a good-humored session, not at all like you might expect if you'd never experienced it yourself. Every week, I whisper to Brian, one of my fellow dancers, 'Go and tell that bloke he's spilt your pint.' It's a joke, particularly because I sense very little violence in that room.

Then they leave and we begin our dance. As we go through body parts, I catch sight of the karate group out in the lobby, getting dressed again, staring in at us and joking and shaking their heads. They're probably saying, 'Oh the old ravers are in again,' but maybe they're not. We're all on a path, after all. Karate is a path.

Their path is about focus, intent, discipline and surrender – and so is ours.

In our circle, the music begins to move us.

'As always, begin by feeling your connection to the earth. Taking deep breaths from the belly, breathing in light and positive energy, breathing out tension and negativity. And then move your focus, first of all, to your head. Let it go ...'

All through the body parts, then into the wave of the five rhythms. The ever-moving circles of flowing leading to the percussive strikes and thrusts and lines of staccato; letting go of the head to fall into the madness, the abandon of chaos; picking up the jumps and skips of lyrical, feeling the heart lift into joy and then, finally, transforming into the radiant energy of stillness, that full emptiness, that slow, measured vitality. Still the mind, release the emotions, free the spirit. Not dancing to the music, but with it, in union with it, my body part of a whole, making love to the music, the magical, synergistic combination of diversity, my own diversity, all the way through the wave. I look up into the light as the music fades, my body stopped but inside of me the wheels are dancing and singing. Still the mind, release the emotions, free the spirit. A moment of eternity, and so *alive!* No-one to impress, no-one to influence, no-one to negotiate with; no-one to please, no-one to close down, no-one to pretend for. Nothing to plan. Nothing to buy, nothing to read. Nothing to do but be alive. To be here, and now. How can I describe it to you? A feeling: yes. A feeling of peace, of calm. Yet a feeling of vibrancy, of passion too.

I know that feeling now.

Time has passed in all our stories, and I'm still dancing.

Four years have flowed by since I first met Heather on that sunny afternoon at the IOD. As I look back over that time, it seems an incredible series of coincidences, mistakes, interruptions and unpredicted outcomes. Has it guaranteed me success, power and riches, like the self-help books I once read suggested they could? No. Am I free from mistakes, and the old dark emotions and habits that drain energy – self-doubt, anger, envy, self-sabotage and the like? Absolutely not. A long time has passed, a lot of work has been done; but sometimes I feel like I have only just set out on the journey. What I do know is that I am developing the capacity for catching myself out. I try not to allow myself to indulge in old habitual behaviors which served nothing and nobody but my ego.

What else has changed? I can say that I am more optimistic than ever before, since everywhere I look I see potential rather than limitation. I am more passionate to change things than I used to be, but also more patient when things do not turn out as I hope. Understanding the dark side can be as satisfying as transcending it.

I am more tolerant and less judgmental of others, since I understand the value of diversity and the damage that standardization can do. Above all, I feel more connected – connected to other people by being able to listen better, connected to myself by following my heart and intuition more. (It was my heart, and not my head, which urged me to tell this story.)

As a result of this integration, many of the separations I had set up in my life have dissolved. I don't think, for example, about 'bringing work home', since I see now that all life is work of a sort. Not the work of travail and burden and labor, the work that was handed down by God to punish our original disobedience – but the inner, sacred work of discovery and learning. Life may be work, but the balanced consequence of this is that my work – work work – has more of life in it too.

Finally, I understand organizations from an utterly different perspective now. Companies do not suffer from many different problems, each unique to the situation, as I first thought; they suffer very few. And the problems they do face are merely reflections of those faced in the personal lives of the people who work there. The battle is not won and lost on the organization chart; it is carried on in our souls.

As I sat and waited for Heather at the airport coffee lounge, I found myself doodling on the pad in front of me. Some things, I thought, have not changed.

Heather and I were about to fly out of London to speak at various conferences on the teachings of the Business Recapitation Wheel and the potential for us all to find the sacred in business. Since the workshop in Wales, we had worked together many times. This was the first time we were to work apart again, a necessity brought about by a growing demand for our messages.

Could I have anticipated that this would be one of the results of letting go of my old life? Had I imagined it could ever bring me to this point? No.

Face your fear, and trust. Make space for magic.

I wrote Heather's words.

This was a time for looking forward, but also a time for looking back.

Discover ...

My pen was writing more now, not doodling. Could I sum up what I'd learnt?

Discover who you are by finding out first of all who you are not. Identify how you were molded and sculpted as a child, what armor you're wearing to protect you from fear – and therefore happiness. Find out what masks of pretence you are wearing – at work and outside life – and ask yourself why you are wearing them? What's the cost, what's the benefit? What are the outcomes? And make sure that the mask has not become you. You'll have spent a large amount of energy in supporting your ego over the years. Why not use that energy for the real you?

The only way to the light is through the darkness. But work on your own darkness with humor, with fun. Not with guilt.

Open your mind to what experience is teaching you – don't close it in with dogma, assumption or laziness. Live from the heart. Listen to the hunches of your body. Find and recognize your connection to All Things through Spirit. Find balance.

Find your sacred dream, the work that brings you pleasure, and touch others with that gift. "Dance your dream awake".

I had no sooner written down Heather's words when she appeared at my table.

'God, Bill,' she cried, dropping her bags to the floor, 'I need a coffee!'

She looked like she'd been up all night and had not bothered going to sleep.

'Good morning, Heather!' I smiled, with exaggerated energy. It was 10 am. Too early for an owl to be flying. I brought her a large dose of caffeine and waited for her to come to. We sat in silence for a while, after which she went to buy us two more coffees.

I looked up at the departures board, checking the flights to Amsterdam and Los Angeles. Heather came back, definitely more awake now.

'So,' I asked, 'has the Owl any last words of wisdom before we fly off on the next stage of our journey?'

Heather looked at me. 'Oh, thank you Bill,' she replied, with heavy sarcasm. 'Ask me for a great closing line when I'm still asleep.'

I didn't say anything, but waited.

'Are you really serious?' she said.

I nodded.

'OK,' she murmered, sipping from her cup. 'Let me see. What's appropriate to this moment? What, out of all the stuff I've learnt, do I want to leave you remembering?'

She looked off into the distance for some brief moments, then suddenly back at me. 'I know,' she smiled.

The flight for Amsterdam clicked over from *Wait in departure lounge* to *Go to gate 17*. At exactly the same time, as if the changing notice board had activated a switch somewhere, the airport tannoy crackled into life, and the clipped, English voice of the announcer reminded us that it was important for our safety and security to keep all our personal belongings with us, and only to smoke in the designated areas.

I glanced back down at Heather who was looking at me. I realized, with a sudden blush of embarrassment, that I'd missed what she'd said. I smiled back at her and nodded, looking thoughtful. I guessed it was not appropriate to say 'pardon?'

'Time to go,' she said.

We both stood up and I helped Heather gather up her bags. She picked up her wooden briefcase from the table, and we walked together towards the seventeenth gate.

The Business Recapitation Tour. Day one.

Heather drops her bags onto the bed of the hotel suite in Amsterdam and briefly considers worrying about her session tomorrow. But then she thinks better of it.

From the desk, she picks up an envelope and reads the note inside. 'Ms Campbell, we hope you have had a comfortable journey and enjoy your stay in our city. We have followed your colleague's instructions and given you the cyber suite that he said you would require. We look forward to your presentation in our conference tomorrow.'

'Cyber suite?'

Heather walks over to the TV and then notices its Internet connection, the games console and fax machine. And lots of access points.

I'm four thousand miles away in the States but I'm listening for her laughter when she gets the joke. Heather has nothing to plug in, and no desire to.

I'm also due to speak tomorrow but I'm in a different sort of accommodation. A hotel, but one with spacious rooms of wooden floors, walls and ceiling. No phone, no TV, no monogrammed towels. To my astonishment, I realize that this room has nothing to indicate that it is a hotel – no notices on the bedside table or behind the door, no brands or logos or icons to identify who owns this space. It is, in fact, deliberately and utterly empty of noise and clutter and society. It is a beautiful, warm, soulful place to be. Through my huge bay window, I can see the trees dance in the late afternoon breeze, and I can see the mountains. Grandmother Earth.

In Amsterdam, Heather sighs, shakes her head and smiles.

I take out my bowl of smudge.

THE DEER TRIBE

For further information on the Deer Tribe, write to:

Deer Tribe Metis Medicine Society
PO Box 12397
Scottsdale
Arizona 85267
U.S.A.

Lodge of the Singing Stones
37 Humphrey Road
Sheffield
S8 7SE
U.K.